HEALTH VISITORS AND GROUPS

Politics and practice

Edited by

Vari Drennan, SRN, HV Cert, BSc, MSc
Lecturer in Health Studies, Southwark College, London

Heinemann Nursing

Heinemann Nursing
An imprint of Heinemann Professional Publishing Ltd
Halley Court, Jordan Hill, Oxford OX2 8EJ

OXFORD   LONDON   MELBOURNE   AUCKLAND

First published 1988

British Library Cataloguing in Publication Data
Health visitors and groups: politics and practice
1. Health visiting. Group work
I. Drennan, Vari
362.1'4

ISBN 0 433 00033 3

For Flora and Adam Drennan

Typeset by TecSet Ltd, Wallington, Surrey and printed in
Great Britain by Biddles Ltd, Guildford

Contents

Contributors

All of these contributors are health visitors and have written about their experiences while working in that capacity.

Anne Cross, Co-ordinator, Bayswater Family Care Team.
Gill Denniss, Health Visitor, Bloomsbury Health Authority.
Vari Drennan, Lecturer, Southwark College.
Sarah Forester, Health Visitor, currently living in Kenya.
Diana Moss (née Balter), Community Health Worker, Nottingham Health Authority.
Pauline Pearson, Research Health Visitor, Newcastle Health Authority.
Carol Pittaway, Senior Nurse, Tower Hamlets Health Authority.
Jean Rowe, Lecturer, Croydon College.
Carol Sinker, Nurse Specialist, Tower Hamlets Health Authority.
Jean Spray, Acting Head of Health Promotion, Paddington and North Kensington Health Authority.
Pat Wickstead, Senior Nurse, Brent Health Authority.
Anne Wood, Senior Nurse, Tower Hamlets Heath Authority.
Christa Wynn-Williams, Health Visitor, Granton Community Health Project, Edinburgh.

Preface

This book aims to challenge, inform and aid the development of health visiting practice. It offers the opportunity for practitioners, students, managers and educationalists to objectively examine health visiting practice in the light of changes in demography, the NHS and in community nurse organisation. The book argues for a change in focus in health visiting practice towards an increased use of group and community work methods.

The case studies in the book provide stimulating examples of how health visitors have used group work to identify and address the health needs of their communities. These examples provide role models and opportunities to profit from the authors' evaluation of their work. They also identify their professional requirements such as support, resources, and training in order to work in this way. The last set of case studies actually describe how group work can be used to address the needs of health visitors themselves in enhancing their professional practice.

The final section of the book offers very practical information to complement the experiences described in the case studies. It incorporates ideas, examples, checklists and useful reading for practitioners who wish to add group work to their repertoire of professional skills. The issues that are addressed throughout the book are relevant to other groups of nurses working in the community — and will be increasingly so with the advent of community nurse teams.

If health for all by the year 2000 is the aim of community nursing then health visiting must develop new strategies. For some this book might be a starting point, for others it will be a source of confirmation but, for all, it will provide stimulation and inspiration.

Vari Drennan
1988

Acknowledgements

This book is the result of discussions and debates with many health visitors from all over the country, particularly through the network of the Radical Health Visitors' Group. It could not have happened without the support and opportunities provided by the Health Visitors and Community Nursing Management in Paddington and North Kensington Health Authority over a number of years. In particular I want to acknowledge the support, time and help given by Dave Curtis, Jane Langham, Maureen Kane, Wendy Farrant, Jean Spray and Karen Greenwood.

1

Changing Health Visiting Practice

The debate surrounding the role, function and practice of health visiting has been going on for more than three decades. In the past 15 years this debate has become more critical as a result of the changes in society, changes in the National Health Service (NHS) and changes in people's awareness and perceptions of health and the health services. Health visitors have been questioning their practice in the light of these changes. If the health visitor is a 'family visitor' advising all ages from the cradle to the grave, why in the face of increasing numbers of elderly people had the national figures for visits to people over the age of 65 decreased by 12% between 1979 and 1982? If health visitors are concerned with 'individuals, groups and communities' why is there so much emphasis on work with individual women and young children? If the reality is depressed, isolated women, imprisoned in their flats from fear of racial attacks, how is a health visitor to mobilise community resources to prevent ill-health? If low income prevents people from having an adequate diet, what is the health visitor's role in promoting health?

The questioning was (and is) not just about with which sections of the population the health visitor should work, but also how she should interact with them, promoting good health and preventing ill health. In seeking solutions health visitors are increasingly investigating methods of working with groups of local residents and other professionals as a way of complementing their interactions with individual clients.

This chapter examines the changes in our society which have led to this questioning of practice; the changing focus of health visiting towards working with groups and the issues that need to be addressed to facilitate this change of focus.

CHANGES IN SOCIAL PATTERNS

It is important to be clear at the outset how social patterns have dramatically changed, as this provides the context within which health visitors are reappraising their traditional priorities and practices. In this section the main changes in demographic patterns will be examined, followed by an account of the changing patterns of health.

Population Trends

The total population has remained fairly static since 1971; however the population age structure has changed. There has been a decrease in the proportion of children aged 15 and under, and an increase in the proportion of people aged 65 and over. These patterns are projected to become more pronounced as we move into the 21st century. The population aged over 75 will have increased by 750 000 by 2001; those aged over 85 will form 12% of the elderly age group, compared with 7% in 1981 (Central Statistical Office, 1984). Linked with these changes there have been changes in household and family groupings. Between 1961 and 1981 the proportion of individuals living alone increased from 4 to 9%, forming 23% of all households. Likewise, the number of single parents (mostly women) has doubled in the same period to 5% of all households. Over the same period the divorce and remarriage rate has increased.

The pattern of migration has also changed. Although 90% of the population lives in urban areas, cities and large conurbations such as Merseyside, Tyne and Wear and Greater London have seen a decline of 5–10% of their population between 1971 and 1981. Since the mid 1960s migration from the UK has been at a greater rate than immigration (Osman, 1985). In 1981 just over 3.25 million British residents were born outside Britain. Only one-fifth of the black and Asian population aged between 17 and 64 were born in Britain in 1981, while 85% of black and Asian children aged under 16 were born here (Fothergill and Vincent, 1985).

Employment

Another major demographic change has been to do with patterns of employment. Britain now has more registered unemployed than at any time since records began. From 1971 to 1979 the number of people registered as unemployed rose from 0.8 to 1.3 million. Between 1979 and 1983 the number of registered unemployed people jumped to 3.4 million because of the accelerated rates of inflation and recession. The pattern is now one of long-term unemployment from an earlier age. In 1971 there were 20 500 unemployed school leavers; by September 1984 214 600 school leavers were unemployed (Fothergill and Vincent, 1985). In April 1984 almost one-fifth of unemployed men had been out of work for between 1 and 2 years and a further quarter had not worked for over 2 years.

For those in employment there have been changes in the patterns and conditions of work. The number of part-time employees in Britain increased by 34% between 1971 and 1981, although the total number of employees fell by 2% over the same period. It is noteworthy that in 1981 only 6% of male employees worked part-time, compared to 42% of female employees (Central Statistical Office, 1984). The electronics industry has been one of the few growth points in the British economy and the application of new technology is increasing rapidly. Although the silicon chip has opened the way to new production methods, it has also reduced the need for staff, particularly unskilled staff, and presented a new range of occupational health hazards for those employed.

Income

While the wealthiest 5% of the UK adult population owned slightly less of the marketable wealth in 1981 than in 1971 (41 compared to 52%), 680 000 people lived in families with incomes below the supplementary benefit level — that is, below the 'officially accepted' poverty line (Central Statistical Office, 1985). Many observers (see, for example, Townsend, 1979) have argued that this level is set so low that anyone whose income is up to 40% higher should be considered to be living in or on the margins of poverty. In 1981 28% of the total population were within this definition of poverty and families with children made up 44% of this group — a sharp change from 1979 when elderly people formed the largest section (Graham, 1985).

Other factors have led to marked changes in social patterns. Perhaps one of the most marked is the reduction in spending on renovating old and building new houses, most notably in the public sector. One result has been the steady increase in numbers of households accepted as homeless and in priority need by local authorities. In the first half of 1980 33 170 households were accepted as homeless in England, compared with 35 700 households in the first half of 1982 (Osman, 1985).

Health Trends

All of the above socioeconomic factors have implications for the health and well-being of different sections of the population and as a consequence have implications for the planning and delivery of health services. The Black report (DHSS, 1980) has shown unequivocally the association between low socio-economic class and increased incidence of mortality and morbidity. It demonstrated that the poor health experience of lower occupational groups applies at all stages of life. Further to this, the report pointed out that this gradient, instead of being reduced since the inception of the NHS, has stayed the same and in some cases steepened. A recent review has shown that serious inequalities in health have persisted into the 1980s and that the occupational class gradient of increased mortality and morbidity has actually steepened since 1979 (Whitehead, 1987). The report and this latest evidence throw into relief questions about the nature of health service provision, together with the material conditions necessary for good health.

However it is not just social class that has an impact on health experience. The adverse effects of unemployment on health have recently been highlighted. The unemployed and their families have considerably worse physical and mental health than those in work (Whitehead, 1987). The association between old age and increasing chronic illness has long been recognised (Grimley Evans, 1981). In 1978 one-third of all people using hospital beds and two-thirds of disabled people were aged over 75 (DHSS, 1978). The poorer health experiences of black and Asian people as a result of racism combined with overall low socioeconomic status is beginning to be acknowledged (Torkington, 1983). The effects of homelessness and temporary accommodation on adults' and children's health is beginning to be documented (Drennan and Stearn, 1986). The patterns of mortality and morbidity have altered during the 20th century. The infectious diseases which were the scourge of maternal and child health and the focus of much health visiting activity have given way to different causes of ill health and death which need new responses from health visitors.

CHANGES IN THE NHS

A second important contextual thread is that of the changes that have occurred within the organisation and financing of the NHS. NHS finances rose annually until the mid 1970s when the rate of increase became substantially smaller. If allowance is made for the demographic changes, trends in demand and technological innovations, then this smaller increase actually became a 1% decrease (Butler and Vaile, 1984). In 1982 for the first time there was no planned increase in the real resources of the NHS. Since then resources for growth have been expected to come partially from efficiency savings and have not taken account of annual increased spending from demographic changes. In 1984 the first staffing reductions in the NHS were announced.

Against this background of decreased investment, there have been three major managerial and administrative reorganisations in the NHS. In 1974 the Community Health Councils (CHC) were created, giving the consumer a means of reacting to management decisions in the health service for the first time. The overwhelming experience of staff within the NHS has been of a period of change, and more recently uncertainty about the future. These reorganisations have taken the administration of community nurses out of local authority control, into community health service management and more recently, for some, into hospital management control. In the same period a variety of government documents have introduced and promoted a number of key concepts encapsulating changes in health care philosophies (see DHSS 1976a, 1977, 1981). These concepts include a devolvement of health care to the community, an emphasis on providing care for priority groups such as mentally handicapped people, a focus on self-help and individual responsibility for health and an interest in community participation.

Critiques

Inextricably woven in with the changes sketched above has been the growing number of critiques on the health services. These critiques focus on a variety of areas and come from a range of sources — politicians, health professionals, carers, consumers, feminists, economists, sociologists and social policy makers. They can be summarised under the following headings:

1 The applicability of the medical model of health and illness (McKeown, 1976; Kennedy, 1981).
2 The role of high-powered technology versus the role of prevention (DHSS, 1976b).

3 The power and social control aspects within the role of health professionals, particularly doctors (Illich, 1975; Zola, 1975).
4 The unequal distribution of health care both intra- and inter-regionally (Yudkin, 1978; Butler and Vaile, 1984).
5 The unequal access to health care services between people of different social classes, races and gender (Doyal, 1979; Brent CHC, 1981).
6 The emphasis on prevention as an individual responsibility as opposed to a collective or social responsibility (Crawford, 1979; Mitchell, 1984).
7 The split of management functions between health authorities, family practitioner committees and local authorities and the lack of co-terminosity in many areas (Health Visitors Association, 1985).
8 The lack of opportunity for consumer participation within the health services (Klein and Lewis, 1976).
9 The lack of democracy and accountability within the health service (Thunhurst, 1982).
10 The hierarchal nature of medical care (Salvage, 1985).

These critiques are apparent in many different formats, not just in the examples given above. They can be seen in government papers and reports during the 1970s and 1980s and in the manifestos of all major political parties. They are apparent in the increasing interest and use of complementary and alternative therapies, in the formation of self-help groups and in the growth of pressure groups for specific services, such as well woman clinics. They are also reflected in the growth of resource, information and campaigning organisations, such as the Women's Health Information Centre, London; the College of Health; the London Health Democracy Campaign and the local Health Emergency Campaigns. The formation of groups such as the Association of Radical Midwives and the Radical Health Visitor Group is also the result of such critiques.

These criticisms come from all parts of the political spectrum and illustrate the dramatic increase in public awareness of all aspects of both health and illness in the last 20 years. This means that the health visiting service, as part of the health service, is also under scrutiny. It also means that health visitors are having to look for ways to work with that public awareness, relinquishing the idea that opinions and knowledge rest solely with the health professionals.

THE IMPLICATIONS FOR HEALTH VISITORS

These changes and debates have thrown into sharp relief the critical appraisal of the health visitor's role and practice. Debates that found expression in articles in the 1960s and early 1970s highlighting the uncertainty and questioning of the health visitor's role (Jefferies, 1965; Harwood, 1966; Draper et al., 1969; Hunt, 1972) moved on to a nationwide debate concerning the principles and practice of health visiting (Council for the Education and Training of Health Visitors, 1977). In the late 1970s and early 1980s these debates led to the formation of such ginger groups as the Radical Health Visitors (see Chapter 4, Case study 10) and the call for a government inquiry into health visiting. In formulating their evidence to the inquiry into community nursing in England the Health Visitors Association (HVA) held workshops and meetings nationwide to discuss the future role and practice of health visitors (HVA, 1985).

While envisaging a role that responds to present-day society, health visitors have come to look increasingly to group and community work methods of practice, with their emphasis on consumer-expressed definitions of need. Health visitors are not alone in this change of emphasis. Increasingly, the philosophies of the provision of health care are now embracing the notion of partnership between the professional and individual or community at large. More emphasis has been given to client or community perceptions and definitions of need, participation in planning and active involvement in the provision and evaluation of care. Documents from the World Health Organization (WHO) such as the *Declaration of Alma Alta* (WHO, 1978) and more recently, *Global Strategy for Health for All by the Year 2000* (WHO, 1981) have embodied these principles. In nursing, work methods are being advocated which reflect an increased desire to respond to client- or patient-defined needs, actively involving them in decision-making and care processes in order to improve the social relationships between consumer and provider. The nursing process is the most evident example. While many nurses view it as a new way of record-keeping, one of its main thrusts is of partnership in all its stages, as can be seen from this definition:

The nursing process requires a systematic approach to a nursing assessment of the person's situation, including an evaluation and reconciliation of the perceptions by the person, the person's family and the nurse. A plan for the nursing actions to be taken may then be made with the participation of the person and the person's family and then implemented. Evaluation of the outcome is performed with the person and the person's family (Nurses' Reference Library, 1984).

The implementation of the ideas behind the nursing process can be seen in many areas in the hospital setting (for example, Burford Nursing Development Unit, 1985) and in the community (for example the Bristol Child Development Project, 1984). For the most part this rethinking is concerned with individual nurse–client/patient relationships. However the WHO thinking on community nurses included a much broader scope for partnership:

Community nursing includes family health nursing but is also concerned with identifying the community's broad health needs and involving the community in development projects to health and welfare. It helps communities to identify their own problems, to find solutions and to take such action as they can before calling on outside assistance (WHO, 1974).

This focus on the wider community was taken up and re-emphasised in the definition of health visiting given by the Council for the Education and Training of Health Visitors (CETHV, 1977):

The professional practice of health visiting consists of planned activities aimed at the promotion of health and the prevention of ill health. It thereby contributes substantially to individual and social well-being by focusing attention at various times on either an individual, a social group or a community (CETHV, 1977).

At the same time as health visitors are being encouraged to use community work methods they are witnessing the growth of a wide range of community-based activities, mostly outside the health service, concerned with the promotion of good health. This interest in health by community workers has also come about as a result of the rapid flowering of public interest in health services during the 1970s and 1980s. This interest is exhibited in a wide range of activities: individuals with a thirst for information about personal health; self-help health groups; exercise and fitness activities; groups concerned with the social causation of ill health; the increased interest in and use of alternative therapies, as well as campaigns to save, alter and improve existing health services. Health visitors have only just begun to engage in the debate about different work methods and it is important that this should be continued. In searching for an understanding of what community work methods mean for health visitors it is necessary to examine the world of community work in health itself.

COMMUNITY AND GROUP WORK IN HEALTH

There are many different ways community groups can be formed. They may start as a result of a particular incident, or from the desire of individuals to make contact with others in a similar situation or with the aid of community workers. The professional activity of community work has developed from the belief that people have the capacity to join together to act for themselves and that even in the most depressed lifeless communities this capacity can be stimulated by a small group of well trained and prepared workers. Community work exists 'to help the community as a whole develop skills of collective activity, decision-making processes and management of its own institutions' (Clarkson, 1982). It is concerned with assisting people in achieving social change 'in the area of social conditions and social institutions (London Council for Social Service, 1979). Thomas (1983) has described the work at a neighbourhood level which emphasises the process whereby groups of local residents are assisted to clarify their needs and then take collective action in response to these needs as community development. The origins of community development in Britain can be found in attempts to develop mass education and social welfare in the colonies in the years between the two World Wars (Mayo, 1975). That experience, together with the examples of some of the War on Poverty programmes in the USA, informed British policy-makers (Baldock, 1980) and led to the use of community development workers in the government poverty programmes initiated in the late 1960s and early 1970s, such as the Educational Priorities, Urban Aid and the Home Office Community Development programmes (Hubley, 1980). Descriptions of these programmes, together with critical discussions as to their impact and problems, can be found in *Gilding the Ghetto* (Community Development Projects, 1977) and *Making Sense of Theory* (Halner and Rose, 1980). Traditionally, community work has been concerned with issues such as housing, unemployment, youth work and leisure opportunities. However, it is increasingly recognised that health is a central issue in all these traditional areas and as such has become an area of increased activity for community workers (Community Projects Foundation, 1982).

Community Health Initiatives

'Community health initiatives' is the term used to describe the varied activities concerned with health but usually outside the health services. It has been estimated that there are now more than 10 000 such local activities in existence (Klein, 1984). Rosenthal (1980) was able to pinpoint seven new community health projects in London and a 'flourishing of activity around health issues amongst generalist community workers from London and beyond who have been coming together for over a year to courses and meetings . . . at the London Voluntary Service Council'. Rosenthal identified the features which these growing numbers of projects had in common:

All are based in deprived, working class, inner city areas. All try
to counter the predominant individual and disease-based models of ill health on which our health services are organised,
recognising that ill health is actually created by society in
various ways. Several of the projects use the WHO definition of
health as a primary reference point for their activities . . . All of
the projects employ workers trained and experienced in community work rather than in medicine, nursing or health education to work on health issues in small defined geographical
areas . . . The workers are usually supported by an advisory
group of both local people and sympathetic health professionals
who decide collectively on the direction and initiatives the
project should take.

Descriptions of community-based projects can be found
in compilations (Smith, 1982; Kenner, 1986; Community
Health Initiatives Resource Unit/London Community
Health Resource (CHIRU/LCHR), 1987a), conference reports
(Somerville, 1985; CHIRU/LCHR, 1987b) and reports of
individual projects (Albany Health Project, 1983; Youd and
Jayne, 1987). These record the diversity of work ranging
from campaigns about damp housing (see, for example, the
North Kenton Health Project in Pollitt, 1985), pensioners'
health groups (see Pensioners' Link, Brent, 1984) to challenging inappropriate and inadequate health care (see, for
example, the Hackney Multi-ethnic Women's Project in
Somerville, 1985). The phenomenal growth in these community activities led first to the establishment of the
London Community Health Resource (LCHR) in 1981. This
organisation aimed to link, support and promote discussion
in London. It was followed by a similar national organisation called the Community Health Initiatives Resource Unit
(CHIRU), established in 1983. Both have been involved in
producing newsletters, directories, examining the training
needs of community health workers, assessing evaluation
techniques and organising national conferences to raise the
profile of community health work and attract potential
funders. They have now amalgamated and expanded their
work with funding from the DHSS.
    Within the NHS another group of health professionals has
shown increasing interest in community health initiatives:

health education officers. They have closely aligned themselves with self-help projects and community health projects. Since the late 1970s they have been appointing officers
with community development remits and in the mid 1980s
began initiating community health projects either managed
by or as part of their departments (Drennán, 1986a).

HEALTH VISITORS AND GROUP WORK

Health visitors can learn and are learning from community
work a method of relating directly to a community's experience of health and the health services. Unfortunately many
of those involved in community health initiatives have
already examined health visiting and many have dismissed
it. Probably one of the most dismissive, certainly the most
public was made by a community physician at a national
conference on community development and health (Morris,
1985). He stated:

> there is *no* health service professional with the training, the
> time and experience to do it (community development) . . . Yes,
> I have heard of health visitors — but they will not do . . . All
> our health professionals are just that — professionals with a
> training in a particular knowledge area whose main attribute
> will be that knowledge. In community development we are not
> really talking about the possession or lack of knowledge about
> health, we are concerned more with encouraging people to
> approach and to tackle those issues that concern them.

The debate concerning the differing skills and perspectives of health visitors who are interested in the community
and community workers interested in health is just beginning to be aired publicly (CHIRU/LCHR, 1987b). However
the above-cited statement denies the fact that some health
visitors are and have been very closely linked with the
communities they work with in a wide variety of ways. It is
only now, after 120 years of existence, that these activities
are beginning to be documented.

A Historical View

Both Dingwall (1976) and Robson (1982) have documented the close connection between the Ladies' Sanitary Association (from which present day health visiting originated) and a wide range of collectivist issues, such as franchise and property rights, education and employment opportunities for women. Robson also draws attention to the wide variety of activities that the 'ladies' were involved in as well as home visiting. These included holding public lectures on infant care and household management as well as organising savings clubs for the purchase of coal, clothing and blankets. With the growth of the health visiting service in the early part of this century, talks and classes on child and maternal health, sewing circles, cookery sessions and mothers' groups continued as a feature of some health visiting practices in the infant welfare clinics (McCleary, 1935). The practice of running groups and holding health education sessions in infant welfare clinics has continued since the inception of the NHS. In 1969, Allen *et al.* reported that, of the 157 health visitors in Herefordshire, 29% were involved in teaching in schools, 40% in antenatal classes and 24% in running parent and mothers' clubs. In 1978 Perkins reported that of 120 health visitors in Nottinghamshire, 55% were involved in teaching in schools, 77% in antenatal classes, 34% in other learning groups and 36% undertook 'one-off' talks with youth clubs or adult groups.

Types of Groupwork

Historically it is clear that health visitors have always been involved to some degree with groups of people; however, 'group work' is a term that health visitors use a great deal but rarely define. It seems to incorporate different types of activities. These are:

1   Teaching health education topics to a group of people in a structured formal manner.

2   Sharing health information in a dialogue with a group
    that is already formed.
3   Forming and/or supporting groups for the purposes of
    self-help, mutual support and health information.
4   Becoming part of a group, made up of local people and/or
    professionals, formed to influence policy and/or services.
5   Coming together as groups of health visitors to enhance
    their own practice by sharing ideas and/or mutual
    support.

In any given situation these categories are not mutually
exclusive. However what is clear is that health visitors are
moving further away from the formalised health education
talk in their search for ways of working with people in
addressing the issues and causes of present-day ill health.
Health visitors are increasingly looking to categories 2–5
(above) of group work as a means of supporting and
empowering people in dealing with the causes of ill health
they have identified.

Examples of Health Visitor Activity

While antenatal classes and health education classes in
schools are the most obvious examples of the more formal
teaching of health topics, the intention of this book is to look
more closely at the remaining categories of group activity.
This section merely sketches examples of the different
categories to give some idea of the breadth of health visitors'
activities. The depth of health visitors' activities and
achievements are documented by the case studies given in
Chapters 2 to 4.
    Furlong (1975) provides an example of the second category
(see above), giving a description of her 3-year involvement
with a community-based mothers' group in which she
joined, offering her knowledge in an informal way. It seems
that health visitors form groups with one of two objectives
in mind. These are:

1 For the purpose of support, either informally as in a housing estate coffee morning (Farnese, 1979) or more formally as in a closed counselling group (Hennessey *et al.*, 1978).

2 For the purpose of providing both learning opportunities and support, such as an adult health group (Moulds *et al.*, 1983) or a mothers' dance and health group (Gillmore, 1983).

The majority of groups initiated by health visitors seem to involve women with young children, reflecting the health visitors' case loads. However a growing literature indicates that health visitors are involved in groups of a wider age range and of other interests. These include pensioners' groups, menopause support groups, bereavement support, stop-smoking groups, slimming and exercise groups (Drennan, 1986b).

The fourth category of group work activity (see above) has been described by Kewley (1983), who wrote of her involvement in a successful campaign for a community centre for elderly people in Liverpool. Phillips (1986) has also described her participation in a successful housing estate campaign to provide a family centre with day care facilities in south London.

Health visitors coming together to provide mutual support and ideas for practice is a relatively new idea but seems to be increasing throughout the country. Spicer (1980) and Vizard (1983) have documented the establishment of health visitor support groups, while the Radical Health Visitor Newsletter describes workshops organised to examine specific aspects of health visitor practice.

While the documentation of the actual group work remains relatively small, an HVA survey, conducted in 1984, was able to indicate the wide variety of community groups and organisations with which health visitors have been involved (Drennan, 1986b). These included:

women's groups	luncheon clubs
community centres and projects	family centres
	tenants' associations

youth organisations	homelessness campaigns
neighbourhood health projects	rape crisis centres
women's refuges	active elderly groups
unemployed centres	campaigns for well woman
local voluntary organisations and societies	clinics

In recent years a growing number of health visiting posts have been established which are committed to using more group and community work methods. Health visitors in Brent, Newcastle and Nottingham are working in innovative, multi-disciplinary teams to provide new community-oriented approaches to child and maternal health (Pearson, 1983; Wann, 1984; Billingham, 1986). These are examples of outreach health visitors working alone, without case loads, in geographical areas (Drennan, 1985; Newell, 1984) or as part of a multi-disciplinary team in community centres (Biggs, 1986) or in community health projects (Forester, 1981; Wynn-Williams, 1986).

Influencing Factors

There can be seen to be a growing commitment within health visiting to using these types of group and community work activity. However it would be wrong to suggest that all health visitors are interested in these methods or that they have all always practised them. Hobbs (1973) has argued that group teaching was seen as integral to health visiting activity before 1940 and that after the inception of the NHS it ceased to be seen as a core method of health visiting. Her research showed that the major influence as to whether health visitors became involved in group work was the attitude of their employing authority. She noted that aspects such as the recognition that group work is valuable, the availability of health education resources, the practice of giving time back in lieu of evening group work were all factors which actively encouraged health visitors to become involved in group work. More than a decade later it is clear that the same factors influence the work of health visitors. In the 1984 HVA survey (Drennan, 1986b), health visitors indicated that lack of resources — time, space or money — hindered any group or community activities. The lack of health visiting time, large case loads and staff shortages were specifically identified. So too were health visiting management policies in certain areas which actively discouraged group work and refused to give time in lieu of evening activities. The health visitors also emphasised their lack of experience and skills in group work as a factor that further hindered them.

In the face of such evidence it would be naïve to suggest that suddenly every health visitor in the country will start working with groups of people on health issues. Before that happens health visiting needs to address a number of issues about its professional practice and training.

THE ISSUES FOR HEALTH VISITORS

Group work is a positive method of both enabling people to address health issues they have identified and disseminating health visiting knowledge. Group work activities are complementary to the more conventional activities of health visitors in promoting health. The increased numbers of health visitors embarking on such activities demonstrate that they can achieve results which would be impossible by individualistic methods. They have shown that the use of groups is effective in providing support (Drummond, 1984), establishing community networks (Hiskins, 1983), combating isolation (Cox, 1983), providing general health information (Walters, 1979), giving people the opportunity to share and debate ideas about health (Gregory, 1982), alleviating anxiety and depression (Thomas and Sullivan, 1983) and in fulfilling the need for open informal discussions with health professionals (Drennan and McGeeney, 1985). As a method group work is also an effective means of acquiring much needed community facilities (Phillips, 1986) and tackling particular issues such as stress (Tyler and Barnes, 1986). The case studies set out within this book (Chapters 2–4) document examples of these achievements in greater detail.

However, for health visitors to be confident about adding group and community work to their repertoire of practice certain issues have to be addressed. These issues fall into three categories. These are:

1   The recognition of the legitimacy of group work.
2   The practical needs of health visitors.
3   Evaluation.

The Recognition of the Legitimacy of Group Work

Hobbs (1973) argued that group work was seen as an optional extra for health visitors with a special aptitude. The Royal College of Nursing (RCN) have expressed their surprise at the lack of use of community work methods by health visitors (RCN Heath Visitors Advisory Group, 1982). An examination of health visiting textbooks and professional statements shows that the emphasis has been placed on individual interactions, affording group work a secondary place. It seems there is an undercurrent of feeling amongst health visiting managers and health visitors that needs to be examined — the feeling that group work is an optional extra for when they have completed the real work of health visiting, i.e. home visiting and running child health clinics. At one extreme, group work is seen as undemanding work, an easy option that contributes little towards the true task of health visiting, while at the other extreme, work directed to influencing policies or services is seen as outside the scope of health visiting and possibly dangerous as it may become 'political'. The result of such views is that health visitors can be actively discouraged from adopting or trying such methods of work (RCN Health Visitors Advisory Group, 1982). The discouragement takes many forms (Drennan, 1986b). In some cases health visitor management will refuse to allow group activities to use health service resources, e.g. free clinic rooms. In other cases health visitors will be permitted to become involved in group work provided it is in their own free time. The refusal to allow time in lieu of extra hours worked in the evenings or weekends with community groups is another way in which health visitors have been discouraged from becoming more active. More stringent measures have been invoked, although rarely documented, where health visitors are moved to a different part of the health authority, their case load changed or they are given verbal warnings to cease their activities with community groups. For many health visitors it is the lack of understanding, interest and active support from their managers that is the real discouragement.

The function of health visiting — social police or promoters of health?

It is important to examine these seemingly negative views. When some health visitors say that the true task of health visiting is child surveillance, they are not speaking flippantly. Luker (1982a) has argued that a broadening of health visiting activities to encompass other age groups, such as the elderly, is mediated against because of the increasing pressures on health visitors to seek out cases of child abuse. This pressure also prohibits the development of methods of work outside of home visiting and with a wider section of the community. One only has to examine the pressures arising from such highly publicised child deaths as Jasmine Beckford and Tyra Henry to understand why the service and individual health visitors feel it is their responsibility to be as vigilant as possible — a vigilance that is made easier by home visiting. It is not just health visitors themselves who feel this responsibility; clients and the public at large perceive this to be the main task of health visiting. Research in Glasgow has shown that 56% of the sample of first-time mothers studied described the role of the health visitor exclusively in terms of social control — particularly focused on the policing of child abuse and neglect (McIntosh, 1985). This research reinforces the findings of previous studies (see, for example, Graham and McKee, 1979; Blaxter and Patterson, 1982). This view is endorsed by certain health visiting practices such as calling on people unannounced. Most health visitors do not wish to be seen as social police but as advisers and a source of information and child development experts. However the fact remains that they are a major source of referrals about potential child abuse to social services departments.

There is an inherent contradiction in the health visitor's role that cannot be ignored. However, health visitors themselves have to decide whether they wish to go further down the road to total child health police or whether they wish to move towards being promoters of health for all the community. At the present time there seems to be no simple solution and health visitors will continue attempting to keep an uneasy balance. This difficult tightrope between social police and promoter of health must influence the activities of health visitors with groups. However it is an issue that has not been fully debated. If health visitors are seen to be part of a system that can make judgements about levels of parenting and part of the legal process of removing a child from parental care, can they also be seen as enablers and non-threatening sources of information in the same community? Is it truly possible for the same person to have such a degree of power and also work openly to build up trust and confidence with groups of local residents? Until health visitors begin documenting their work more fully in the light of such issues this whole aspect remains unexplored.

Recognition

The apparently negative view of group work has been supported by the manner in which health visiting is officially evaluated. The assessment continues to be based on the number of people visited at home or seen in the clinics each week. The Department of Health and Social Security (DHSS) only collects and publishes statistics on home visiting and child health clinics sessions; it does not recognise any other methods of working and thus implicitly devalues them. In many health districts, health visitors have devised their own statistical return forms on health visitor activity which include sections such as 'health education sessions' — a sweeping term which both highlights the professional concerns and marginalises any other activity such as forming a support group or acting as an informal health resource at a community drop-in morning. With the implementation of the Korner recommendations (DHSS, 1983), health visitors now have the opportunity of expanding the collection of information at district level to include the wide variety of group and community work they may engage in. However, one of the concerns expressed on the proposals for gathering information about health visiting activity has been the emphasis on case load-related approaches and the neglect of group and community interventions (HVA, 1985).

To describe the more policy-influencing aspects of group work as political and therefore dangerous is a red herring, in that it fails to acknowledge the political nature and implications of all health visiting practice. Spray (1982) has argued that most of the knowledge base from which health visitors make judgements, give advice and form relationships with clients is politically constructed. Health visitors are employed by the government as part of the welfare state — a political construct. Health visitors carry out government policies — again politically mediated. 'The daily decisions about practice and priorities derive not from neutral principles based on objective truths but on political interpretations of the world and identifiable political purposes' (Orr, 1985).

The Practical Needs of Health Visitors

It must be restated that there is an increasing interest and move towards using group work methods amongst health visitors. In order to facilitate that move there needs to be an examination of the health visitors' professional requirements. It has been shown from research that there are a number of important areas — training, time, resources, support and supervision.

Time for group work

In order to emphasise group work activities more positively we have to look at health visiting practice. One problem

which is often raised is that there is no time — that the
commitment of a health visiting case load does not give
health visitors the time to prepare for and work with groups.
There are problems of taking time in lieu of extra hours
worked because of the health visitor's daytime commitments such as clinics, case conferences and liaison meetings.
It seems to take great determination on the part of the health
visitor to use her time in working with groups. In many
ways this is not surprising, given that health visitor staffing
levels have never reached the recommended number laid
down by the DHSS in 1972 (Orr, 1983). This is obviously a
cause for concern if there is to be an expansion of activity.

This raises two questions which seem to be central to the
debate concerning health visiting practice — does there
need to be so much emphasis on home visiting and is
generic health visiting a myth? Can child developmental
screening be done just as effectively with clinic appointments and an increased recognition of the parents' role in
detecting abnormalities, such as with the hearing loss
detection list for parents, produced in Nottingham? Does
there need to be more health visitors specialising in particular types of work, as in some Scandinavian countries?
Would teams of health visitors each with different responsibilities, such as for families with young children, adults,
elders and community group work, be a more effective
resource for a small geographical area? Would the planning
and focus of work be more effective if health visitors were
constantly referring to and updating small-scale community
health and epidemiological profiles, as described extens-
ively by Orr (1985)? Clearly these are questions that must be
examined if health visitors are to work in different ways.

Training

Many health visitors lack the confidence and knowledge to
work with community groups. Health visitor training has in
the past emphasised expertise in delivering a health education talk in a formal, controlled atmosphere. Community
groups are rarely formal or classroom-like. To move forward
health visitors need to explore how to work with people in a

less authoritarian way, which processes are involved in facilitating a group, what are the resources they and the group members can call on and how group work can be evaluated. The experience of being a nurse before becoming a health visitor is based on individual interactions, rarely carrying any sense of working equally with clients/patients, or other professionals for that matter. Many nurses entering health visiting have to undergo the process of unlearning the behaviour of being a professional in a powerful position vis-à-vis ill people who have decisions made for and about them. Much of the learning in health visitor training, as in nursing, comes from observing and imitating experienced trained staff. If trained health visitors are not involved in group work then the student has no role models on which to base herself. The case for observing and learning from people experienced in group work, such as community workers, is very strong. There are also strong arguments for on-going post-basic and in-service training in this field. Obviously there are training courses for group work available. Health education departments, voluntary organisations and training agencies run a variety of short courses on group and community work. However these tend to be short, isolated activities. There needs to be greater provision for regular on-going post-basic courses so that new recruits and newly interested health visitors can train and have opportunities to follow up the initial training. Balter *et al.* (1986) found from their experiences in training health visitors in work with community groups that health visitors needed to explore the following topics:

1 An overall conceptual framework of community development and health.
2 Group work skills.
3 Practicalities in working with groups (premises, crêches etc).
4 Publicity.
5 Working with ethnic minority groups.
6 The use of resources, i.e. audiovisual, written material and group members' own resources.
7 The role of potential helping agencies.

8 The views of health visitor managers.
9 How to set up a group and progress towards autonomy.
10 Evaluation.

They also pointed out that 'effective training in community development work usually consists of a full time 1 or 2 year course, followed by some years of practising and refining skills' (Balter *et al.*, 1986). To expect health visitors to become community health workers who are proficient in community development methods and philosophies after a short course is clearly unrealistic. What the health visitors appeared to gain from the short course described by Balter *et al.* was a greater understanding of the processes involved in working with community groups and the confidence to explore those processes.

Support

In many ways training is linked to support — a generalised term that actually means a number of things. It can be subdivided into the following areas:

Support as in the achievement of practicalities, such as funding for a crêche, a room to use.
Support as in being involved with others — professionals and local residents — to achieve a common aim.
Support as in the opportunity to evaluate critically and scrutinise the work.
Support as in the supervision of the health visiting practice.
Support as in the opportunity to debate and explore ideas.
Support as in the acknowledgement and active encouragement of that work.
Support as in the concern for the emotional and physical well-being of the health visitor.

Breaking down support into these categories shows that there is a diversity of sources from which support should come — managers, colleagues, other professionals, group members and local residents. While the process of being involved in group work should generate particular types of support, there is also a need for support to be built into health visiting practice more consciously than is often the case. Recent research has emphasised the high levels of stress experienced by health visitors, particularly in areas of high social deprivation (Harrison, 1986; Davidson, 1987). The Cumberledge Report (DHSS, 1986) has argued that the ratio of senior nurse managers to community nurses should be 1:15 to facilitate personal support and the development of work. However, health visitor managers also need to have a clearer idea of group work processes to provide personal, practical and evaluative support for their field workers. The managers' need for training and experience in working with community groups is equal to that of the health visitors if they are to be effective. Health visitor practice has centred for too long on the individual health visitor carrying on her own personal work with intermittent consultation with her manager on problems and snatched conversations with colleagues during interrupted lunch breaks. Health visitors need to examine how they can use group work for their own needs. The establishment of health visitor peer support groups in recent years across health authorities are one way this can be achieved (see Chapter 4, case study 8). Another way is the use of health visitor workshops (see Chapter 4, case study 9) where all the health visitors in a particular area gather to view their work objectively and explore new ideas. However with regard to day-to-day practice perhaps health visitors should look more closely at other professionals, such as social workers. Social workers work in teams and allocate time each week to have team meetings during which they review cases, discuss workloads, and share problems. Planning and scrutinising work with colleagues is one way of achieving support. It is of at least equal importance to the execution of the work and should be integral, not an occasional afterthought.

Resources

In networking with other people in a locality and providing more opportunities for health visitors to talk together, health visitors will find it easier to discover what resources are available to facilitate group work. 'Resources' is often taken to mean audiovisual and written materials for health topics but it also means venues, funding, crêche workers, materials to make publicity, people with particular knowledge or expertise and already active groups of people. There is no denying that currently health visitors have little access to funds themselves but they often have little knowledge of who has or how to get access to the funds. The obvious source of material resources and knowledge for health visitors is health education departments and their officers. Unfortunately in many parts of the country this is made difficult by the uneasy relationship between health visitors and health education officers. Health visitors, as users of the health education service, feel that their problems of knowing what services the department has and using the materials it supplies should be acknowledged and responded to — while health education officers feel that it is their decision as to who uses the department, what it provides and how it is used. There are many examples where close working relationships between health education officers and health visitors can instigate innovative and dynamic results in support, resources and ideas. It is important for health visitors embarking on any group and community work to spend time exploring the resources that already exist in their community, as well as the resources available within their health service before negotiating for more resources or access to appropriate ones.

Evaluation

The evaluation of health visiting is an issue of increasing importance inside and outside the profession. As has already been stated, evaluation has previously been within the terms of number-crunching — quantitative rather than qualitative data. Luker (1985) has argued that in the past health visitors have been reluctant to evaluate their work but in the present climate of vigorous competition for resources health visitors now have to generate information about what they do and the outcome. Recent health visiting literature demonstrates the variety of evaluative techniques health visitors are pursuing which encompass more qualitative data. Luker (1982b) has examined goal attainment with elderly women clients. Orr (1980) has examined consumer satisfaction with the health visiting service. Fitton (1981) has studied client response to health visiting teaching. Clark (1983) has described using process and outcome measures in health visitor–client interactions. An increasing number of academics is looking at ways of evaluating health visiting. The Bristol Child Development Project (1984) has developed methods of evaluating health visitor interventions with individual clients and families. Dobby and Barnes (1986) have studied health visitor effectiveness in searching for and dealing with unmet needs. McIntosh (1985) has evaluated health visitor activity from the consumer's perspective.

This upsurge in evaluation research has focused on health visitor activity in relation to individuals: there has been little discussion of evaluative techniques in relation to working with groups of people. As with all health visiting activities, there is more than one purpose for evaluation. These other reasons include:

1 To provide the health visitor with continuous feedback in order to modify and improve her activity.
2 To provide information to the managers for planning.
3 To assess whether it is an appropriate activity for the health visitor.
4 To provide information as to the practical needs of the health visitor.
5 To provide information about the work for a wider audience, both consumers and professionals.

When looking for evaluative techniques it must be taken into account that group work is a dynamic process, not a static contained intervention. Examining community work as a whole, four characteristics have been identified which make evaluation so complex (London Council of Social Work, 1979). These are:

1 The situation is continually changing in any neighbourhood, both physically and in the aspirations of the
   residents.
2 There are both short- and long-term goals.
3 The full implications of the work may not be apparent
   until long after the work is finished.
4 The variables, including the unpredictability of human
   behaviour, cannot be controlled.

These characteristics together with the multiple purposes of
evaluation make it inappropriate to apply the methods of
the physical sciences, i.e. setting up controlled field trials of
a particular intervention, then comparing the outcome with
those people who did not receive the intervention. The
variables would be very difficult to define and outcome
criteria may be far removed in time. The attempts to keep all
variables constant would not allow for modification of
health visitor behaviour as a result of feedback from consumers. Measuring outcome in a manner which takes into
account the dynamic nature of the processes is the subject of
much debate between epidemiologists who prevail in
departments of community medicine and researchers who
follow strategies more aligned with the social sciences.
Some theorists have argued that assessment of health visitor
intervention with a group should be on the basis of speci-
fied individual behavioural objectives, such as the number
of people who give up smoking or lose weight (see, for
example, Luker, 1985). This presupposes that the role of the
health visitor is to change individuals' behaviour via health
education and ignores the fact that the health visitor's role
might be as a resource agent or to enable people to have full
knowledge of a subject on which to make informed choices.
It also ignores the fact that many of the groups with which
health visitors are involved have other aims, such as providing support, building confidence or tackling health issues
that are not within the control of an individual.
   Evaluation techniques based on strategies developed in
the social sciences can offer a great deal in the development
of health visitors. Beattie (1985) has offered a number of
suggestions which include monitoring processes, analysing

clients' perspectives and appraising institutional agendas. Graessle and Kingsley (1986) have broken down the evaluation process in a way which highlights the stumbling blocks for practitioners working with groups. All these propositions offer scope for health visitors to explore them and tailor them to their purposes.

CONCLUSIONS

This chapter has set out the context in which health visitors need to think about their role and consider working with community groups. In order to progress and develop this role serious consideration must be made, not just of material resources such as time and staffing levels, but also of philosophies. To embark upon working in this different way health visitors need to learn not just *from* other disciplines but *with* them. Health visitors also need to learn from and build on the experiences of their own profession. The remainder of the book provides that opportunity. Chapters 2–4 give case studies of how health visitors are working in and with groups to promote health. Chapter 2 describes health visitors' experiences of using group work in health. Chapter 3 relates examples of how health visitors have worked in groups to influence policy and service. Chapter 4 details how health visitors have joined together using groups to examine and enhance their own practice. Finally, Chapter 5 gives basic practical suggestions for use by health visitors who wish to become more involved in working with groups. If health visitors are to have a place in promoting health for all in the year 2000 then there is a need to build on and extend the innovative and exciting work that has already begun.

2

Group Work in Health

In this chapter four case studies are given demonstrating how health visitors are using group work methods in promoting health. The first three are written by health visitors who were involved with a group as well as having an individual case load, while the last is written by a health visitor who worked solely with community groups. These case studies give some idea of the range of work being done by health visitors and indicate how working with groups is complementary to individualised work. They also show how group work can expand and enhance health visiting practice, both in reaching out to a wider section of the community and in the depth of interactions.

Although these case studies describe work carried out in different parts of the country — London, Nottingham and Edinburgh — and each has a different focus, there are several common strands that are important for health visiting practice. The first point to note is the health visitors' own commitment to and enthusiasm about working with groups of people. Moss and Forester both highlight how important this was for their continued involvement, particularly in the light of pressures from case loads and limited managerial support. Of equal importance is the need for support for the health visitor managerially, personally and professionally. Wynn-Williams describes in detail how she used local networks to gain personal and professional support as well as locate resources to facilitate her activities. Moss and Drennan discuss the importance of their local health education departments and in particular health education officers with responsibility for community development. Each of the authors stresses the importance of a close trusting relationship with staff from other disciplines, such as community and social work, for the success of the venture and their own professional development. Forester in particular examines how trust and support were established between her, a social workers and a volunteer who led the group.

All the authors identify the importance of group members participating in all aspects from decision-making to sharing experiences. While the others describe very open community groups, Forester relates her experience of establishing a closed group concerned to address one immediate issue, that of withdrawal from long-term tranquilliser use. Each describes the developmental process and the growth of other activities out of the original one. Drennan writes about individual discussions in groups evolving into a long-term health visitor involvement, which in turn generated a pensioners' health course, then a festival and culminated in a health handbook. Wynn-Williams and Forester lament the lack of formal evaluation but all four authors are able to document indicators that helped them determine the worth of their activities and shape new ones. The evaluation process is clearly happening but it is rarely documented or collated. Evaluation of these types of activities by health visitors is an area that needs a great deal more attention.

Finally, these studies will provide both inspiration and practical details for other health visitors who wish to work with groups of people.

COMING TO GRIPS WITH GROUPS

Christa Wynn-Williams

Edinburgh is well known for its Festival and famous landmarks like the castle and Holyrood Palace. It is also mentioned frequently on television programmes about AIDS. One area in particular, Muirhouse, is often mentioned, together with the depressing statistics which are flashed on to the screen to the discomfort and frustration of local tenants. This part of the Greater Pilton area is one of the housing schemes built after the War and contains a mixture of multi-storey and tenement accommodation. Unemployment, poverty, and ill health statistics, as depicted in the Black report (DHSS, 1980), were factors with which I grew familiar during my first 3 years of health visiting there. During those years I identified the local resources and facilities. Finding out how to gain access to services and understanding the intricacies of welfare rights took up time too. Most energy went into home visiting, meetings, clinics and keeping records up to date. After getting to know the area, I became involved in a women's health group. This study outlines how this happened, the supports and resources used and its evaluation.

My case load was relatively small, partly because working geographically meant that much time was spent with families moving into the area who later joined local medical practices, and partly because many of the houses were empty and redevelopment was expected. Having this smaller case load enabled me to visit the local clubs catering for different needs and age groups. Being invited to talk to groups of mothers or to pensioners gave me some insight into their organisation and management. I learned that the members of these groups did not ask for a talk by a health visitor, nor did they decide on the topic. It was rather that a worker or committee had wondered: 'Who can we invite along to entertain or educate the group?' The topic was inevitably chosen by me, despite my request for suggestions. This is a crucial matter to which I shall return.

In the spring of 1983 two social workers from Family Care, an Edinburgh-based organisation for single parent families, began a drop-in coffee morning session for their clients in Muirhouse and the surrounding area. They invited these women to bring their friends to meet informally over refreshments in the canteen of a social education centre. This building had separate space for a crêche and other rooms were used later. After meeting informally for some weeks the women were encouraged to think about what they might like to do besides chatting. Having heard about these coffee mornings I called by and was roped into a discussion which happened to be about what the women thought about health visitors. The discussion was taped as a way of recalling what was said and 'de-coded' the following week.

Shortly after I was approached by the social workers to see whether I was interested in leading a women's health group. The decision had been made by the workers that the women should be offered a choice of three groups which were to be relaxation and keep-fit, welfare rights, and health. We (the three group leaders, the crêche worker, two social workers and a student on placement with them) met several times to plan these groups and to organise the practical arrangements. The idea was for the drop-in café staffed by the social workers to continue and for the activities to be offered simultaneously in separate rooms. Leaflets were printed and nearly 1000 were distributed through the local primary schools. Only two more women came as a result of this publicity! People respond through word of mouth and experience has taught me the value of learning local networks. The student's role was to assist me in the running of the health group, and she was around for the first 3 months only.

Getting going seemed difficult at the time because there were so many uncertainties, e.g. who would come, what would their interests be, how many sessions would be held, how would the student and I work together, how much time would all the planning take? In retrospect this preparation time should have been longer, and some of these questions should have been answered. Before committing myself to take the group I had consulted with my nursing officer who was very enthusiastic. I was told that as long as my routine family visiting was carried out I was free to take on any group work I wished. Encouragement in this context was in the form of an acknowledgement that there was a need for a different kind of health education from the traditional talk and question time. Reasons for poor attendance at parent-craft classes are much debated, and in this area classes have been discontinued. I welcomed an opportunity to work informally with this very varied group of single parents who had chosen to meet this way. Therefore, my expressing a wish to try something different was welcomed by nurse management.

Having the interest, the time and the encouragement was one thing; having the expertise was another. I thought I knew quite a bit about group work. I had 7 years' teaching experience, I had participated in several groups myself, and I had done some homework in the library. I knew I had a great deal to learn about the skills these women had which enabled them to survive in what was and still is a tough area.

The group met every week for 2 hours. Except for holidays and one attack of laryngitis, I was always there. I have learned since then just how important this reliable, regular commitment was to the group. Many months later we were tackling the problem of late-comers, and I knew I had sometimes been late myself in the early months. I felt ashamed at my own insensitivity in giving the implicit message that the group was less important than my other work, and have often reminded myself of the lesson this taught me.

In the early days, I kept notes and discussed the group's progress at the monthly evening meetings of those involved in this venture. While I was feeling my way I also sought out an adult basic education worker, a community development worker and, much later, a community psychiatrist for in-formal consultation. These people were all a great help in giving me advice and support. Without them I would have given up when problems arose. What I did not realise until much later was how much I needed regular supervision or consultation sessions with someone experienced in group work with whom I could talk over my work objectively.

Making contacts with people in different places was also invaluable to me in another way. By asking around I discovered what the local resources were. Projecting, tape recording and video equipment together with the use of a comfortable viewing suite was available at the local community school. Photocopying was done by Family Care who also found the two salaries for the crèche worker and the leader of a short course I ran for the group. Transport in the form of minibuses was available for rent from the community centre. There are many local sources of equipment, rooms which are underused, and ways of getting materials for use with groups. I found that other workers in the community are keen to share knowledge and experience and have been most helpful.

Discovering who could help me individually and where I could get practical assistance was a beginning. The next stage in my learning was when I was invited to join a group which has now been running for 2 years. The initiative came from two workers on an adult learning project who saw the need for those engaged in adult group work to meet and share knowledge and skills. Called a Practitioners' Skills Exchange, it is a monthly 2-hour meeting aimed at increasing awareness of what happens in groups, learning new skills from each other and providing a 'clinic' time at the end of each meeting where problems can be shared, with the potential for several solutions or ways forward. Participants come from a variety of situations, working with groups concerned with mental health, self-help, literacy and numeracy, oral history, photography, and anti-racism. So far I have been the only health visitor in this group.

Through this monthly meeting I have been able to learn how many of the problems I was having are common to all groups. We had whole sessions of setting up, keeping going, planning programmes, hidden agendas, why groups fail, what tasks need to be shared, and much more. Currently we operate a system of having a co-ordinator, note-taker and observer whose roles are taken by different members each time. The observer reports his or her observations before the end of each meeting and these are discussed. Such activities greatly increase awareness of the group process. This group is a model of every group and provides an opportunity for experiential learning. Because we are all from different agencies and employing authorities it has been possible to talk really openly about difficulties relating to our group work. These could not have been aired so freely at a unit meeting of health visitors where many of those present are not doing any group work.

I shall now describe the two main areas of challenge in this work — training and appropriate back-up or support. In order to function effectively as a group worker specific skills are needed, and being equipped with a basic training in group work contributes greatly to a sense of confidence about starting in the first place. Skills for this work are gained by being a member of a group oneself. Consultancy is required with others engaged in similar work and also on an individual basis. Sharing information with colleagues is definitely not enough. Learning the hard way can be so painful that it can lead to discouragement and a yielding to the kind of cynicism which I have met, typified by comments such as 'It's been tried before', 'These groups don't work . . . people always stop coming', and 'You're welcome to try, but what's the good?'

How can the effectiveness of a group be measured? This is never easy. Looking back over the ground covered, I noted how often the most lively sessions have been about relationships, about feelings towards children, and the joys and trials of being a parent. Also extremely helpful were the sessions of role-playing on the possibility of talking to children about sexual abuse — almost a rehearsal ground. The realisation that lack of confidence was a common shared experience led to an 8-week training course in assertiveness. This enabled many women to discuss their feelings more freely because of the insight they had gained into their own behaviour. It had an immediate benefit in helping some become more confident with their children and some began using the crèche for the first time. Previously they had been unable to do this, and our sessions had been hampered for months by the presence of bored and distracting children.

Confidentiality is crucial. As trust grew in the group, problems were discussed openly, and it was clearly established that nothing shared would be discussed outside with anyone else. Sometimes I would be asked by a health visitor or social worker how a client of theirs was getting on in the group, and my reply was always the same: 'I cannot comment about your client; discussing any group member would be a breach of confidence.'

The crudest measurement of success would be to ask: 'Was it worth it?' For me, in terms of learning, undoubtedly; for the women attending the group, their own answers have been varied. Some kept coming for the 2 years I was involved, and asked me to continue. Others came erratically, and some came once or twice only. From the outset the Family Care team have had regular reviews with the participants in the project and feedback has always been positive: 'Yes, we enjoy the group because we have made friends, learned more about how our bodies work, and about how to cope better with the situations we meet as parents/friends/ lovers.'

Had I known more about group work when I started I would have been more aware of the need for evaluation. Perhaps the main learning was for the group members to be involved in setting aims and objectives, and in measuring how nearly these were achieved.

Throughout the life of the women's health group I was aware of the fact that in the beginning it had been thought to be a good idea to have a health group, and for social worker–health visitor co-operation. I was also aware of feelings of having put the cart before the horse — of having taken the women where we thought they should go, so the tension was always there. Had they been involved in the planning those tensions would not have existed. However, hindsight is not something one can acquire before the event. It was well worth all the worries — and a great deal of fun!

CASE STUDY 2

LOOKING BACK TO A WOMEN'S HEALTH GROUP

Diana Moss

I first became involved with the women's health group after two women in Eastwood approached the health clinic. It was their wish to test the level of interest in the area for a women's health group and to extend the numbers of those who were already enthusiastic. Meeting informally with this group I explored with them what they wanted to do and how to set about it. It was apparent that the group would accept me as an interested woman (with a knowledge of the health service and with nursing experience) who was willing to work with them on a democratic basis, rather than a health professional there to dictate. The initial meetings took place at the local volunteer bureau and in my own time, which probably served to reinforce my interest with them.

Also attending these discussions was the community social worker, who had been responsible for encouraging these women to make contact with the health workers in the area. She had recognised that their social conversation usually turned to the things that most affected them as women, e.g. bringing up children, menstruation, conception, childbirth, menopause and other health-related problems, and had suggested that perhaps a women's health group could provide an ideal forum in which to discuss these subjects more widely.

During these early meetings the women suggested that an introductory course focusing on experiences of childbirth could run as an attempt to meet some of these health needs. Childbirth was a topic on which they felt they had much to contribute and at the same time would interest other women isolated at home with young children. This initial group of four or five felt that the use of the clinic room after the well baby clinic would be an ideal venue for part of such a course, where interested health professionals could share in the discussions.

My role began by helping with the negotiations towards this course. Firstly, I sought directions from my line manager, who I anticipated would be able to guide me in working with this group (I was a fairly newly qualified health visitor). My line manager was open to meeting with group representatives to discuss their plans. After ensuring that I would accept responsibility for the use of the premises she supported a letter of application from the group for the use of the clinic rooms. Once the use of the clinic premises had been sanctioned I then had to prepare the office manager for this unconventional use of the clinic rooms and kitchen. Although she was familiar with antenatal classes and well baby clinics, where the public were seeking professional advice, she was dubious about a self-sufficient group which was not run by an NHS professional.

Despite this, the 6-week introductory course went ahead in June 1983. It featured films which had recently been shown on television and had stimulated discussion, namely *The Miracle of Birth* and *Natural Childbirth* by Dr M. Odent. These films were shown separately the first and third week with a discussion about them the following weeks. On the fifth and sixth week the women were invited to chat about any health concerns they had and to share ideas on what topics they would like to discuss. This helped to plan future meetings.

The success of the introductory childbirth course led the expanding group to plan future meetings based on the needs and interests they had identified themselves. The areas they wanted to explore were listed and discussed and eight main categories emerged:

1 Relaxation.
2 Stress and mental health.
3 Menstruation and premenstrual tension.
4 Conception and contraception.
5 Nutrition.
6 Cancer.
7 Sexuality.
8 Minor women's problems.

Obviously these areas were too vast to cover in one or two sessions and with my guidance it was decided that a monthly topic would be more realistic, allowing time to deal with each subject in depth. When should the next course start? It was already mid July with summer and school holidays approaching. September appeared to be the best month to aim to begin. The order of topics, rendezvous, care of pre-school children, advertising, arranging speakers and resources all had to be discussed and organised. Weekly summer meetings allowed time for this.

The order of topics was debated and decided on by the group, consideration being paid to the fact that being relaxed and coping with current stress was a prerequisite for the rest of the course. Other factors included school holidays and time of year.

The 6-week introductory course was held alternately in the health clinic and Willow Lodge (a property owned and let to the group by MENCAP). It was envisaged that both meeting places would be used for the next course. However, there was a reallocation of clinic rooms and a feeling amongst group members, health visitor and social worker that the Willow Lodge setting (in the middle of a large housing estate) was more appropriate and convenient for the women. This led to the group meeting permanently at Willow Lodge.

It became apparent that a separate play group would be necessary for preschool children to allow their mothers uninterrupted participation. During the 6-week childbirth course the play group had been run by a volunteer. She had managed the play group well, but felt that she would like to participate in the group's sessions herself. An alternative scheme for child care was discussed. It was decided by the group to approach two young men from the volunteer bureau who had been on play scheme and play leader courses to run the play group. This they agreed to do.

The group decided that they needed some rules relating to discussions and a set way to deal with problems that might arise. It was unanimously agreed that the subjects of politics and religion were not to be discussed, but any other health-related issue was acceptable. An open arrangement for talking through a decision or expressing disagreement with it enabled the group to reach a satisfactory decision in every case. Group participants sharing in the decision-making process was an important feature. No one was pushed to take on responsibility if she did not feel capable and willing.

An invitation to commitment which was declined was not frowned upon. Group members had various talents which became apparent, but everyone appreciated that stresses and outside family pressures did not always make the individual willing to offer her services on every occasion. The professionals working with the group did so with emphasis on the fact that they were not there to run the group, but had certain expertise on which the group could draw. On occasions when both professionals were absent the group functioned perfectly well.

Sharing the work presented co-ordination difficulties in the invitation of outside speakers, arranging dates etc. The group came to recognise this as a problem quite early in its existence and found a phone list was invaluable. The phone list not only provided contact when arranging speakers, but developed as a support line for mutual help during the week.

Advertising the existence of the group had been by word of mouth, hand-written posters and leaflets. The leaflets were designed and printed with help from the social worker. It was a group decision to issue a monthly leaflet. On the front were featured the group's name — 'Women's Health Group' — and that month's topic, while inside were printed planned future meetings and a short background to the group. On the back cover there was a map showing the venue.

Leafleting was carried out by group members and distribution covered the clinic, GPs' surgeries, the library, local shops, post offices, churches, the volunteer bureau etc.

Each monthly health topic was explored from various angles to give as broad an insight into each topic as possible. To achieve this, speakers from a variety of standpoints were invited to talk, i.e. health visitors, Workers' Educational Association, self-help groups etc.

All organised sessions were followed or interspersed with open discussion sessions which allowed time for everyone to air their opinions, hopes and fears and to share experiences. These breaks also allowed time for group members to discuss more pressing health problems.

The health visitor's contribution to the group consisted of a 1-hour introductory session at the start of each of the monthly topics. In the succeeding weeks I shared in the open discussions and guest speaker sessions, and finally evaluated the month's activities with the group.

Generally the aim of the introductory sessions was to introduce the subject, giving an elementary outline of the influencing factors involved, e.g. simple anatomy and physiology. This enabled the group to develop a basic understanding of the topic and be well prepared to go on to learn more about it in the succeeding weeks.

In these sessions I provided relevant films, models, examples of contraceptives, health education leaflets and posters for them to examine and discuss in the relaxed security of the group. At the end of each month the group put together a composite poster to reinforce what they had learnt and to provide a resource for reference in the future. The composition included news clippings, photographs, articles and comments relevant to the specific topic.

During the open and discussion sessions I acted as a generalist health agent for the group, clarifying areas of confusion and misconception, and suggesting relevant points of contact, health screening etc. Sometimes the queries related to other speakers, old wives' tales or newer 'urban parables'.

Over a period of time I became sufficiently well known to be asked simple questions, which I suspect most would not have felt were important enough to contact their health visitor or other health service professional about. This facility was particularly appreciated by those attending the group who were between the age of 16–20 and 40 and above, who had no contact with a health visitor at this point in their lives. This was a valuable contribution which I felt I could make. Referrals which resulted from the sessions included: self-referral to family planning sessions, marriage guidance, the Community Health Council, counselling and GP.

Support, Resources and Time

Within my clinic base the health visitors I worked alongside were generally encouraging. They all visited the group at one time or another and (nursing) students were given the opportunity to come to the group if they wished. Colleagues were sufficiently enthusiastic to offer holiday cover whilst I was away. They encouraged clients who they felt might benefit from the group to join and passed on any appropriate resources they came across. Participation in planning and running a workshop for health visitors on alternative methods of working (September 1983) also produced support from other health visitors within Nottingham and nationally.

One of my firmest areas of support was from the health education officer responsible for community development. He had personal experience of setting up and encouraging health groups and was very positive in his feelings towards the promotion of this type of work. I was able to meet with him to discuss how the group was developing and to talk through what was happening within the group, my role and that of the other group members. He understood the problems that emerged and helped me to recognise the positive outcomes. He had had first-hand experience of similar work and was thus able to suggest appropriate resources from within and outside the NHS that I had not necessarily considered.

He understood the structure I was working in and was appreciative of the constraints on my time. In addition he had visited the group to run a session on 'stress management and control'. Thus he knew the group and had an appreciation of the total situation. I always knew that I could telephone him if I had a query, and that he would generously give time to deal with any problem thoroughly.

Resources within the group were found not only by the members themselves using their own experiences, but also from their collection of appropriate literature, press and magazine articles for the session. In addition there were material resources available from the Health Education Department (films, books, posters, leaflets and models). Finally there were other agencies such as libraries, the Council for Voluntary Service and the Nottingham Self-Help Team who were able to suggest speakers on specific health topics, or refer to appropriate agencies for printing etc.

The time I spent preparing and delivering my introductory session and meetings with the health education officer (community development) was accepted as health visiting work time, whereas the other three sessions (open and discussion) were not.

Management Support and Reaction

There appeared to be some management apprehension about my involvement with the group. There was definite support for me to undertake the introductory formal teaching sessions. However, the open sessions, which involved indirect and informal teaching, information exchange and support for individual, were queried. It was during these open sessions that much of the individual development was begun. Members were encouraged to take responsibility for their own physical and mental health.

The general principle that health visitors should encourage their clients to take responsibility for their own and their family's health is accepted, but the way in which the health visitor actually carries this out is not well defined or established.

At this time there was the added complication of the reorganisation of two separate health districts into one. This involved changes in managers and the unification and implementation of new policies and priorities which naturally take time to become established.

I was encouraged to participate in a study day on self-help groups, but in retrospect, it might have been of greater value to visit other health visitors involved with similar groups. It was this personal experience of working with groups which the health education officer (community development) had to offer.

Evaluation

Success in this form of preventative work is not easily measured; the various reasons who individuals choose to meet as a group are complex and difficult to analyse. Individuals found companionship and empathy from the opportunity to communicate with others. In this environment they were able to learn together and from each other's experiences. In turn this mutual support increased individual confidence. Individuals developed their personalities and embarked on new ventures: Open University Courses, new jobs, weaning themselves off tranquillisers and sleeping tablets, etc.

Increasingly I felt that I was being seen as a useful resource on which individuals could draw, rather than as a health authority agent. Group members extended their new knowledge to those outside the group and encouraged others to use the group and health visitor for specific crisis periods. Daughters introduced their mothers to the group and vice versa.

Interest grew in developing specific subgroups focusing on premenstrual syndrome, the menopause and postnatal support. Group members visited individuals who felt unable to get out to the group and the previously mentioned phone contact provided a useful means of help and support.

Eventually group members were able to help others in neighbouring communities to set up their own groups in response to requests. An explanatory booklet was produced giving detailed information which it was felt could be of use to others embarking on a similar venture.

The group has continued to meet regularly since its beginning in 1982. I understand from my recent contacts with it and with my colleagues still working in Eastwood that it continues to meet successfully.

CASE STUDY 3

A TRANQUILLISER SUPPORT GROUP

Sarah Forester

The tranquilliser support group I was involved with was formed when I was working in a GP attachment in Inner London. The idea for the group evolved from two separate initiatives. Firstly the GPs with whom I was working were reviewing their prescribing policies and offering a withdrawal programme to all of their patients on repeat prescriptions of minor tranquillisers. However, they quickly realised that the withdrawal process was more involved and the patients needed more support than they were able to give in a busy surgery. They felt that the patients needed some kind of relaxation techniques and asked if I knew of anything suitable in the area.

At the same time, the local social work team had started to work on a neighbourhood basis and were keen to be involved with and initiate group responses to local problems. We (GPs and two attached health visitors) had started to meet them on a monthly basis to discuss areas in which we could work together. The social workers had identified stress on local people due to social, financial and housing problems as an area in which they were getting a lot of referrals and felt that individual work was increasingly inappropriate.

After further discussion it was agreed that if we were to set up a support group for those people withdrawing from tranquillisers, this would be a starting point, in terms of collaborating more closely as professionals and finding an appropriate response to the social stresses we all perceived were affecting our clients' health.

A planning group was established, consisting of myself, a social worker, a social work student, the volunteer organiser from social services (whose main responsibility was supporting local self-help groups) and the senior social worker with responsibility for mental health. We held a series of meetings to discuss our ideas and think about the aims of the group, how it would run and what support the group leaders would receive from whom. After the first meeting we were joined by a volunteer who was a yoga teacher. I was already meeting the GPs weekly so was able to feed in their ideas and keep them informed of progress.

It was agreed that the group should be run during the day, should be weekly for 8 weeks, should be closed, i.e. after the first 2 weeks no new members should be allowed to join, and that the first few weeks at least should be well structured. The time given was 2 hours, to be organised as arrival, coffee, informal discussion of problems, experiences of the previous week, followed by a focused discussion introduced by one of the group leaders and then 45 minutes' relaxation.

It was decided that I, the student social worker and the yoga teacher should be group leaders. We arranged to meet the rest of the planning group after the first session, half way through the course and at the end to discuss progress and for support.

We spent some time looking for suitable premises. Although there was plenty of space in the GPs' premises, we were keen that the group should not be associated with a medical response. Finally we found part of a disused children's home which social services contacts negotiated for us to have free. It was ideal in that it had a small sitting room with attached kitchen and a larger carpeted room with a supply of blankets for relaxation.

During the planning stage we took part in a sample relaxation session run by the volunteer yoga teacher in her home. This was important as it meant that the three group leaders got to know each other better as well as how we each worked. I found this particularly helpful as I had never worked with a volunteer and it developed a trust between us. It also meant that we were able to explore the philosophy behind relaxation and agree on its political dimension. Basically we felt that relaxation enabled people to be more in control of their lives and respond to stress in a positive way. This empowered them to change things rather than turn all outside stresses inwards on themselves. Once we had established this core theory, it was easier for us as group leaders to feel confident in each other, although our approaches were different.

Also during this time we read up on tranquillisers, withdrawals and related issues. We got useful information from MIND, Release and TRANX. Health education bought a supply of leaflets from these sources. Finally we began contacting potential group members.

All group members came from GP referral, and we were also given names by other health visitors in the area. All referrals were contacted in writing with a leaflet about the group and asked to come to see me or the student social worker to discuss the group. The leaflet was quite light-hearted (with cartoons) as we wanted to establish that the ethos of the group was as 'normal' as possible and avoid any psychiatric or therapeutic overtones.

Fourteen referrals were seen; eight of these agreed to come to the group. For some the time was inconvenient and others did not like the idea of a group. Those referred by other health visitors were not getting support from their GPs and had not made a decision to try and withdraw. We felt that these clients were not ready for the group but gave their health visitors more information so that they could support their clients in any decision to withdraw. The student social worker and I saw some of the referrals who did not want to come to the group again.

Eventually five people became regular group members. Of these, three were women and two were men; the age range was from 28 to 61. All had been using tranquillisers for more than 5 years and all were determinedly cutting down their dosages slowly.

The programme we had mapped out was agreed by the group members at the first meeting and in the latter weeks of the group they brought up ideas for discussion. At the first meeting we also established the confidentiality of the group. I felt it was important that the relationship between the group and the GPs should be made clear so that group members did not feel that we were reporting back to the GPs or vice versa.

Areas covered during the course of the group included information about tranquillisers — their effects, side-effects and withdrawal; physiological effects of stress; nutrition; assertion; role play of difficult situations; alternative medicine and use of leisure.

The first session went well although we (the group leaders) were pretty nervous. The only problem we had was finishing the group. After the relaxation we allowed people to sit around and one member started to talk at great length about some very personal problems. This was obviously making the rest of the group uncomfortable, especially as it was the first meeting. It was quite difficult to stop her talking. One group member needed encouragement to come again. After this we decided to make it clear that after the relaxation everyone should leave promptly.

We had no problems in the following weeks and had some interesting sessions. We had no difficulty in getting group members to participate in discussions or activities and had a lot of fun as well as some challenging arguments.

After 8 weeks members had mastered the relaxation techniques and the group had run its natural course. One member was keen to continue but this was due more to his need for social outlets. We put him in touch with the adult education department and the volunteer organiser saw him with a view to his doing voluntary work.

There was no formal follow-up of group members which, in retrospect, I think should have been done to evaluate the group. I saw most of the group members when they visited their GPs and the GPs had good reports of the group from them. The planning group had a final meeting in which we discussed what had happened and future plans. We all agreed that, if nothing else, it had been worthwhile for us to join forces in a group approach and that we had learnt from each other's respective skills. We also felt that we had worked out a 'package' on stress management that could be useful in other areas. The local community centre which had a thriving parents' and children's group had expressed an interest in running something similar on a weekly basis with child care facilities.

The GPs learnt more about tranquilliser withdrawal from the experiences of the group members and were keen that a more open group should continue to which they could refer patients as a preventive measure, rather than resort to prescribing again.

Other health visitor colleagues had become more aware of tranquilliser problems and had started to bring up the subject in work with their clients.

Personally I felt I had learnt a lot from running the group. Although I had done extensive group work before and felt fairly confident about my skills in this area the groups had always been in relatively safe areas such as women's health, childminders' groups and antenatal work. This was a new area and had the overtones of group work in a psychiatric sense, with terms such as 'closed group' which I think health visitors have always been in awe of. The support of the senior social worker for mental health was very helpful. I had also never worked as a joint group leader or with a volunteer before. The time we spent in the planning stage was invaluable in making this kind of collaboration a success. In my opinion there are areas of preventive health work with this age group where group work within a GP attachment could really broaden the scope of health visitors' work, thus in the long term avoiding some of the problems we now encounter when visiting the elderly. This group illustrated the whole range of problems which affect people's health outside the medical model and health visitors have much to offer in this area.

My management did not support group work as a health visiting technique except in antenatal and post-natal work, the emphasis being strongly on individual work with the under-5 age group. It was only my personal enthusiasm for group work combined with my slightly isolated situation in a GP attachment that encouraged me to get involved in the first place. My immediate nursing officer at the time was a colleague who was substituting for the nursing officer; she more or less told me to carry on but keep quiet about it! I felt all my other work had to be done before I could run the group, which was seen to be a 'luxury'. This meant that pressure of time was constant during the weeks when the group ran and I did not always arrive at the group as well prepared as I might have been. The other pressure I experienced was the guilt of having such a small group of people take up such a large part of my week. This guilt could have been assuaged with a more supportive attitude from management. I am convinced that the benefits to the group members and the spin-off effects described above made it a worthwhile use of my time.

WORKING WITH GROUPS OF ELDERLY PEOPLE

Vari Drennan

This is a description of the work I carried out with elderly people as part of an innovative research project. The project was established by Paddington and North Kensington Community Nursing Services to examine how a health visitor could work with existing community groups to promote awareness of health issues. It was designed to explore the use of community work methods in the practice of health visiting and to document the achievements, problems and needs of a health visitor working in this way. The ideas and questions behind the project were not merely concerned with the debates about the role of the health visitor but also with the demographic and epidemiological information available about this inner city health district. Paddington and North Kensington health district has been cited as the second most socially deprived district in the country (Department of Environment, 1983). Its population reflects the inner city trends of increasing proportions of young adults and very old people, with a cosmopolitan mix of nationalities. Many factors, including the nature of housing, age distribution and the district's position in central London, contribute to a very mobile population which changes homes frequently. Although few health statistics reflect the general well-being of a population it is possible to get a picture of some of the health problems from the mortality and morbidity statistics. Deaths from cirrhosis of the liver and accidents are more than twice the national average for men, while women suffer twice the national average of deaths from bronchitis and lung cancer. The district has the third highest tuberculosis notification rate in the country and the two boroughs it covers have the highest suicide rate in England and Wales (Paddington and North Kensington Health Authority, 1985). Against this background the Community Nursing Service management was seeking new ways of working for health visitors which would address the health needs of the entire community, not just women with young children.

I, as the research health visitor, aimed to work with groups of people in a way that acknowledged and responded to their perceptions of health and illness, viewing people in a holistic way rather than as a set of compartmentalised problems, such as overweight or bronchitic. It also meant that in working with groups of people there were opportunities to look at the common threads in health issues rather than individualising problems. In establishing the project, experiences from other community workers and particularly from the health education officer with responsibility for community development were utilised. As a result the project had a number of organisational features which are unusual in health visiting. Although I remained a part of the health visiting service, there was a steering group comprising people with skills in community work, health education, research and health visiting. From this group, which met infrequently, was formed a subgroup which met more frequently to look critically at the work I had done and offer advice and support. I was based within the health education department to facilitate access to its resources and particularly to draw on the support and expertise of the health education officer with responsibility for community development.

What did the title 'health visitor with community groups' mean? In essence I worked just like any other health visitor — I knocked on doors and offered my services as a health visitor. However, the doors I knocked on were those of community organisations, not of individual households. I did not have an individual case load. I offered myself to community groups as a resource to look at health issues. I wanted to avoid being the unknown guest speaker who delivered a lecture to a passive audience and then was rarely seen again. I aimed to build up a relationship with the group, find out in what respect the group members wanted my expertise and then work with them in the way they chose.

During the course of the project I developed work with 23 groups. Although the emphasis was on working with existing groups because of time constraints, I did become involved in establishing two community groups (Drennan and McGeeney, 1985) and in planning and participating in a number of local events. All the groups I worked with reflected the multi-cultural, predominantly working-class population of the health district. Although I worked with a wide range of ages (Drennan, 1987) in this case study the focus is on my involvement with groups of elderly people and in particular how that work evolved.

Initially I visited a number of pensioners' groups and organisations in one part of the health district to introduce myself. As a result of these visits and my conversations with the group members I was invited to return to lead one-off discussions on certain health topics. These individual sessions were a way for me to begin to get to know the group and a basis from which to develop more activities. The topics ranged from rights in the health service through bereavement to living with arthritis. Out of these individual sessions I came to work closely with several groups of pensioners over a period of time. The slow developmental process cannot be over-emphasised. Groups have their own particular time scale and life span which are always affected by incidents in people's daily lives — accidents, deaths, holidays, encounters with authorities etc. In talking with the group members we planned other sessions or even series of sessions of their own choice. In all of these encounters the emphasis was on sharing of knowledge, information and experiences. I brought my health visitor's knowledge and they all brought at least 60 years of experience and learning.

To illustrate what happened I will summarise my involvement with one group — a housing estate pensioners' group. I was originally contacted by the estate community worker who had heard of me from another pensioners' organisation. He invited me to come and meet the pensioners' group who were keen to know about their entitlements in the health service. From this first meeting, which was nearly a month after the original phone call, the group decided they wanted to talk about arthritis. Then they wanted to talk about medication, then emergency situations, and so it went on at intervals throughout the year. Although they chose a particular topic, inevitably the discussions included many different aspects, either as a result of something that had happened to a group member that week or because of their own experiences. For example, the discussion on medications turned to examining feelings about sleeping tablets and why people used them; the discussion on emergency situations centred around the experiences of several of the women whose partners had unexpectedly died in the home and one who had awoken to find her husband had died in his sleep. The discussions inevitably drew from common experiences which affected their health. These experiences included expensive heating, high noise levels from other flats, fear of being mugged in the lifts and corridors, rubbish and furniture being thrown out of the windows of the high-rise flats and loneliness and isolation. These were issues that were talked through providing comfort and reassurance. Often plans were then made with the community worker to try and deal with the problem, such as lobbying the council or keeping an eye out for frail people living alone. It was a very positive move when the group members went from analysing a situation to having the confidence to act on it as a group.

An important point to make is that as well as the entire afternoon being spent with the group a lot of time was needed to plan and prepare the sessions. The time taken to prepare for my input included reviewing videos, making and producing handouts (which incidentally usually had to be of large print with clear colour differentiation for those with poor eyesight or who had not brought their reading glasses), telephoning to confirm dates, arranging for help with carrying equipment such as a TV and video recorder, and thinking about how to introduce a topic as well as facilitate discussion and participation. At least as long as the session itself went into planning and preparation.

Evaluation was an integral aspect of the work, providing feedback into the process, and has been described more fully elsewhere (Drennan, 1985). Monitoring activities, analysing group members' views, and identifying immediate effects influenced the decisions about my future activities. It became clear that local elderly people wanted opportunities to discuss health issues in informal settings with the involvement of a health professional. The more I made myself known and the more I became involved with pensioners' groups, the greater the demand became for me as a health visitor to participate.

In trying to respond to this need and develop the work further I, together with some pensioners and a worker from a local pensioners' organisation, planned and held a short health course for elderly people. It was held in a local health centre and was very successful. All the organisational tasks were shared amongst the planning group, including deciding on the topics, inviting speakers, producing and distributing posters, encouraging people to come and borrowing relevant books from the local library to lend to participants. The topic areas were: how our bodies work, relaxation and massage, food, what to do in an emergency, and aches and pains. The sessions were held weekly in a room chosen for its easy access. Each included exercise or sports and a teabreak. Each afternoon was attended by up to 25 people and the discussions were very lively. Even those who only joined in the gentlest of exercises became visibly more supple and more confident by the end of the course. All of the library books were borrowed and on returning them the borrowers were keen to discuss what they had read. From this health course people with particular needs or interests were introduced to other agencies and permanent groups in the area. It was hoped to repeat the course in other parts of the health district but unfortunately the project was not long enough to allow this.

Additional research funding however allowed me to develop this momentum which my role had been instrumental in creating. The obvious interest in health amongst elderly people led to the suggestion of a major health festival in North Kensington. The planning process was long and complicated and involved pensioners at every stage. It had to include organising volunteers, transport, access aids to all parts of the venue (an adult education institute), to name but a few aspects. The festival itself was a day-long event. There were workshops, information stalls, refreshments, activities and sports. Among the workshops available were those run by a district health authority member, a local GP, an osteopath and a beautician. Stalls offered the chance to discover more about statutory organisations such as social services, and voluntary organisations such as Pensioners for Peace. Funding from the Greater London Council and Age Concern allowed us to subsidise the lunch-time meal, pay volunteer expenses and produce publicity in three languages. The festival had many results, for example: people joined groups, such as a yoga group for elderly people; a group for Spanish elders was established; some pensioners' groups started health discussions and the district health authority member gained first-hand information from pensioners on their views of the health service. In discussions afterwards with elderly people who had attended the festival it became clear that it was seen to be very valuable. The planning group felt it was important to document the event in a way that would be accessible and useful to people in the community rather than as a report that no one would ever read. So through charitable funding the planning group produced a health handbook for pensioners in Kensington and Chelsea based on the activities of the festival and illustrated with photographs from it. The handbook was distributed free at post offices and through community organisations. There was a very positive response from elderly people to its production.

This project demonstrated the vast unmet need for this type of work by health visitors. It showed how community group activity is complementary to health visiting focused on individuals, as it reaches out to wider healthier sections of a community. It also highlighted how important support, multi-disciplinary co-operation and access to resources are for health visitors working in this way to be effective. As a result of this pilot project the Community Nursing Services have now established a permanent post of health visitor with community groups.

3

Working in Groups to Influence Policy and Services

In this chapter are detailed three case studies which describe how health visitors have joined with other people to influence policies and services. All are very different yet together they give a valuable insight into the variety of methods that health visitors are using to respond to health needs. The first two case studies are written by health visitors who are part of multi-disciplinary teams; the third is by a health visitor working from a clinic base. Cross relates how health visitors helped to establish a drop-in centre and advice project for homeless families living in bed and breakfast accommodation. Pearson describes a health visitor's role in changing the nature and emphasis of child health services in a multi-disciplinary team. Denniss and Wickstead write of their participation in a community's attempt to get a new, much needed family centre.

As in Chapter 2, these case studies are from different parts of the country and focus on different health needs but they have common themes running through them. The first theme is the recognition of health needs. Cross and Dennis and Wickstead relate how their recognition of need came from talking to local people in their case loads and from the collection of statistics. Dennis and Wickstead mention the use of surveys and questionnaires in trying to establish people's health needs. Pearson narrates the experience of a project that was established as a response to epidemiological evidence and which then worked to involve the users much more in defining their own health needs.

Each case study highlights the way in which these health visitors established a network of contacts, both lay and professional, which facilitated a response to the acknowledged health needs. Cross has documented the importance of such a network in finding resources, skills and support to influence provision. Pearson writes of a wide range of work and changes in services which came about through working with people from other disciplines. In conjunction with the building of a network of contacts in a community, Pearson and Denniss and Wickstead reaffirm the value of working in a multi-disciplinary team. The value is seen not only from the consumer's point of view but from the health visitors' — they gain support, access to different perceptions and opportunities to develop their work in promoting health in many different ways.

Denniss and Wickstead and Pearson stress the importance of working within the framework of educating student health visitors and other health visitors. Each provides opportunities for students to observe her work over differing periods of time. These authors stress the worth of providing role models for students to imitate. Denniss and Wickstead also emphasise the value of having an on-going dialogue with educationalists.

These case studies give concrete examples of how health visitors work with other people to achieve the principles of health visiting, which are:

1   The search for health needs.
2   The stimulation of the awareness of health needs.
3   The influence on policies affecting health.
4   The facilitation of health enhancing activities (CETHV, 1977).

They also point to some of the problems experienced by health visitors when they work in this way. These difficulties include having to examine the power relationship between lay people and professionals, the low level of understanding of such activity amongst the health visiting community, and the stresses created by confronting the tension between visiting individuals and working to find a collective solution to common health problems. In documenting their activities and achievements in such detail these health visitors have provided a source of inspiration, a wealth of practical information and much food for thought.

COMMUNITY ACTION: PLANNING A FAMILY CENTRE

Gill Denniss and Pat Wickstead

We will briefly introduce and describe the team we worked in for 5 years and then give one detailed example to illustrate the kind of work we were involved in during that time. Our work load encompassed two large existing case loads with primary health care team attachments, a geographical area, the need to plan for the development of joint work with our social work colleagues, and the fostering of self-help groups.

The original concept of the neighbourhood project evolved out of discussions between a senior health visiting manager and a local social services area manager. Many needs had been identified by health visitors and social workers based in this area and the hope was that an integrated team approach would avoid duplication and improve communication and co-ordination of services, thus providing a better service for clients.

The housing estate was built as high-rent council housing in the late 1960s. In 1971 it became normal waiting list housing and in a comparatively short time 70% of new lettings were to people from homeless families' accommodation: 60% of the population of the estate were from ethnic minority groups and over 50% were single parents.

Team members of the project included social workers, two health visitors, community workers, family aides, an under-5s worker, and a home care team for the elderly. We gradually developed a team identity with a commitment to a community development approach and challenged the assumption that social work and health visiting could only operate with a service delivery style of work. An example of this type of work was our involvement in the planning of a family centre on the estate.

Ever since the estate had been built it had been recognised among professionals that there were inadequate community facilities. This, coupled with a vulnerable population of many isolated parents of young children who themselves had had poor parenting experiences, not surprisingly resulted in high numbers of receptions into care and physical and emotional abuse. The figures for children considered to be at risk at that time were amongst the highest in Brent. Existing day care facilities in the area were already over-subscribed and in many cases suffered from inadequate premises, equipment and funding. There were also no opportunities for parents to meet informally to share experiences.

As professionals we had also identified the need for a centre as a base for therapeutic group work activities, demanding a high level of both professional and parental involvement.

During the course of our research we visited several family centres in London. The underlying philosophies and facilities varied but the staff we met shared the conviction that community participation in the planning of a centre was vital to its success. Such participation led to greater acceptance in the neighbourhood and a higher uptake of the available resources within the centre. With this in mind the original steering group of ourselves, a senior social worker, a child-minding development worker and a community worker contacted local community groups and advertised an open meeting to raise the issue. Over a period of time we held regular meetings, circulated a questionnaire and produced a display which was used during an under 5s week based in the health centre on the estate. This display was also incorporated in a consultation exercise with the local community, looking at the future planning of resources for the estate.

At the same time, we and the senior social worker in our team prepared reports for the social services management team and for various committees of the council. At a local level we endeavoured to engage with head teachers, community workers and local GPs, as well as with our own colleagues. We also lobbied local councillors and invited them to meet with us in the hope that they would then be conversant with all the issues and support our proposals through the different committee stages.

We became increasingly aware that there were constraints and conflicting demands for finances for such a project as ours and therefore we needed to demonstrate that we had fully researched the cost implications. This included preparing estimates for capital and revenue requirements and also alternative sources of funding, e.g. urban aid, European Economic Community funding or a joint Health and Social Services budget.

Another important task was to meet the local authority architect and initiate a feasibility study. From the findings of the tenancy questionnaire we identified a site which would be acceptable to the local community in terms of its position on the estate and the inclusion of essential outdoor play space.

Our experiences of working in a multi-disciplinary team convinced us that the proposed staff for the family centre should include different professionals who could offer a broad and varied approach. Most of the centres we had visited had been set up and staffed in the main by a single professional body, namely social services, and were managed by that agency. We identified a range of skills that would be required by staff and these included: administration; development work (how to set up and service groups); child care and parenting; education and leisure activities; group work. Part of the costing exercise involved working out salaries, how to price specialised equipment, transport etc.

An essential part of our work was the need to communicate with and keep informed the various management hierarchies at every stage. It was also essential that we let the various community groups know the latest developments and encouraged them to contribute their ideas. One particular example of this was during the under 5s week. Because of the focus of the week and the opportunity to sit and talk with young parents, we were able to explore and test out our ideas and measure the value of the multidisciplinary approach using a variety of activities. We also gained more ideas and feedback from parents not previously consulted because they were not part of a recognised community group or did not feel able to complete the questionnaire or attend a public meeting.

Following the success of this week we identified some immediate needs and were able to offer some short-term resources. For example, we started a toy library, a supervised play session at a weekly child health clinic, a mother and toddler group and a 'parenting' group run by a social worker, a health visitor and two family aides. We envisaged that these activities would eventually be incorporated within the family centre and that we would have gained valuable experience in working in different ways with parents and young children.

Obviously to undertake such a project as this was time-consuming and demanded a great deal of energy. Some of the difficulties were to do with the cumbersome and often slow decision-making processes associated with the organisational structures of both the local authority and the health authority. We were frequently frustrated by pursuing ineffectual lines of communication and were often thwarted when other projects were deemed to be of more importance than ours. These decisions often seemed to be made by people who had no local knowledge of the community and its needs and who made no effort to meet with us to discuss issues. One of the biggest disappointments was the lack of interest shown by our own health authority, as we felt it would have been an ideal initiative for the joint care planning team to support.

One of the difficulties of working in a non-traditional way is the risk of being misunderstood and undervalued by your peers. It took patient and well reasoned arguments to justify that what we were doing was adopting a different yet valid approach to meeting the health needs of the local community. We felt it was essential to enlist our health visitor colleagues' active support both to promote the idea and also to sustain us during this time.

We encountered similar difficulties in our relationships with health visiting managers. Whilst we were not greatly discouraged from pursuing this initiative, we would have welcomed more active support and interest, especially at meetings where decisions were being made about allocation of resources. Our need for regular supervision and, for example, help with the necessary prioritising between our ordinary health visiting work load and this community development work was not recognised. At times it was extremely stressful trying to make the right decisions about the effectiveness of this type of health visiting in the long term, when often the immediate needs were more pressing. Another useful role of the manager in this situation would have been to defuse the tension that existed between other health visitors and us and to demystify and validate our approach to our work.

The area of work that we felt least prepared for was related to reaching out and engaging the local community. Because of the complicated dynamics of communities it is difficult to ensure that a representative cross-section is consulted and even harder to gauge its response.

We found that some groups and individuals who were initially very committed to the idea of a family centre were unable to sustain their commitment. There were a number of reasons for this, including lack of appropriate child care arrangements for meetings, people moving from the area, unwillingness to come out after dark because of the risk of violence and of course previous experiences of disappointments and unrealised expectations. As with many communities there were a few people who, because they were willing to be involved in community action, were at risk of being overwhelmed by the heavy demands on their time and we were not always successful in sustaining this group's interest and energy.

Another area of conflict was the confusion that arises when different agencies or individual workers compete for scarce resources. In our naïvety we thought that, as workers on the estate, we all had a common goal. The particular difficulty we encountered was a campaign for a community nursery which became confused with and ultimately in competition with the family centre project. We originally identified the need for a community nursery and in fact initiated the campaign and believed that this was as essential as a family centre but serving different needs. However this concept was not grasped by influential members of the council or by some senior managers in social services.

The team in which we worked provided our main support both on a day-to-day basis and in the long term. With a commitment from all team members to a community development approach there was no need for us to explain or justify this particular piece of work. We were encouraged, supported and fed new ideas during regular team meetings. The whole issue of group work was the subject of many discussions and the focus of one of our study days. We questioned the status of this style of working, discussed the difficulties and identified the value of adequate supervision and training. One of the ways we tried to tackle some of these problems was to form our own support group for those of us engaged in various forms of group work. This forum provided us with the opportunity to explore ideas, gain more insight into group dynamics and gave us the momentum to carry on when morale was low. Other practical and invaluable support from the team was help with leafleting, making posters, collating questionnaire findings, acting as crêche workers and even making the tea.

We also gained support and ideas from other workers engaged in similar activities who we learnt about or who had contacted us through different networks. These included other health visitors working in innovative ways, either in health authority posts or as community workers in health projects. We were interviewed by *London Health News* (Wann, 1984) which resulted in our participation in a workshop at a conference focusing on community development in health (Somerville, 1985). We found these opportunities stimulating and supportive and were encouraged to learn of other initiatives in different parts of the country. Another positive aspect of such contact was the chance it provided for us to share our experiences and promote our non-traditional approach to health visiting.

The fact that we were both field work teachers enabled us to have a dialogue with educationalists concerned with health visitor training. We believed that health visitor students benefited from an unusual multi-disciplinary placement and were able to share the experiences they gained with their peers at college. The interest shown by lecturers was greatly welcomed as they could easily appreciate the philosophy behind our work and encourage the students to adopt these principles in their future practice.

In summing up, perhaps we could begin by giving an update on the family centre. The time taken from the original idea for a centre to the final submission of plans to a full council meeting was 2 years. Unfortunately political events beyond our control (when Labour lost its overall majority) resulted in the rejection of our proposal along with many other community initiatives. We are hopeful however that this resource will materialise since the political situation has changed yet again. Also in Brent people are currently more aware of the value of a facility of this kind following the events around the death of Jasmine Beckford.

Although we have both moved on to different jobs we feel we have gained invaluable experience and are able to continue to develop our work in the ways we have learnt and can encourage others to do the same. We feel that health visitors are ill-prepared for such a style of working, particularly in trying to understand large organisational structures and processes. On a practical level we have little training and few resources to lobby, pursue fund-raising possibilities, and write persuasive reports using appropriate jargon. Health visitors are not alone in feeling inadequate when it comes to engaging the community and we should look at working more closely with community workers, voluntary organisations and others who may have more training, experience and expertise in this field.

We believe that health visitors are the ideal community health workers. We can be proactive and stand as advocates in the neighbourhood in which we work and should be facilitators in those communities, identifying needs and campaigning for resources.

CASE STUDY 6
RIVERSIDE CHILD HEALTH PROJECT
Pauline Pearson

The Riverside project, as everyone locally calls it, began life in 1979 as a purely medical initiative. It was primarily a response to the Court report (DHSS, 1974) but one which also tried to take into account some of the issues which the Black report (DHSS, 1980) was soon to raise about inequalities in health and access to health provision.

The original aims of the project as set out in September 1979 were:

1   To provide extra medical input for children in an inner city area where child health needs are unusually high and child health services are unusually stretched.
2   To assist in the integration of services for children in this area, both within health services and between health, social and educational services, and in particular to encourage the provision of comprehensive child health care within general practice.
3   To encourage families and the local community to assume a greater share of the responsibility for the health of children.
4   By working within the area, to learn more about the needs of children in a disadvantaged area, bearing in mind especially the educational responsibility of a university department of child health towards medical, nursing and other professionals, and to develop a community resource for undergraduate and postgraduate training.

The boundaries of the project were chosen following discussion of a study carried out in 1975 and 1976 to examine the distribution by electoral wards in Newcastle of various indices of childhood morbidity and mortality (Downham et al., 1980). This showed that three of the four wards in the Riverside area (see Fig. 1) ranked in the worst four in the city on a scale combining measures of perinatal

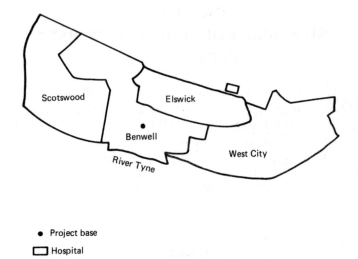

● Project base

☐ Hospital

Fig. 1 Riverside Child Health Project area (showing ward boundaries)
Reproduced by kind permission of the Bayswater Homeless Project

mortality, low birth weight, deaths between 1 week and 2
years, respiratory syncytial virus hospital admissions, and
hospital admissions for non-accidental injury. Three of the
same wards also featured in the top five in a survey
produced by the social services department in 1974 (City of
Newcastle, 1974) which looked at the incidence of adult
unemployment, adult crime, mentally ill case load, rent
arrears, electricity cut-offs, take up of free school meals, and
children in care.

The four wards which were chosen have a population of
around 40 000, with a high proportion of children (16.7%),
of which a high proportion live in single parent households.
The wards contained at that time 13 primary schools, two
secondary schools, two special schools, four nursery schools
(and 12 nursery classes), two social services day nursery/
family care centres (one with residential accommodation),
three social services offices, three clinics, one health centre
and 14 general practices. Twelve health visitors and five
school nursing sisters worked in the area.

Historically the area expanded during the 19th century
when ship-building and armament manufacture were thriv-

ing along the River Tyne, and thousands of terraces of flats were built, running up the steep banks in parallel rows. Latterly, during the 1960s and early 1970s, many of these terraces were demolished, to be replaced by a mixture of low-, medium- and high-rise council properties, together with some rented by housing associations. Heavy industry has largely been replaced by warehousing, with a consequent huge reduction in jobs, though one firm retains a factory, building tanks along the river side.

At first, funding was derived from three main sources: Newcastle University Department of Child Health, Newcastle Area Health Authority (as it was then), and Inner City Partnership. Five doctors (including three in short-term rotational training posts) and two secretaries moved, early in 1980, into a base in a local infants' school. They had two rooms, later increased to three as work with local people began to require more space. From the earliest days of the project it was clear that a wider membership of the project team was needed in order to fulfil the agreed aims. In Autumn 1980, Save the Children Fund commenced supporting the project, employing a director of social and community work and establishing posts for a further community worker and a secretary through Inner City Partnership money. Shortly afterwards, in February 1981, the health authority seconded a health visitor (the author) to the team, also through Inner City Partnership funding. Save the Children Fund later also established a part-time information worker post.

There was a shift from university to health authority funding in 1982 with some consequent alterations in medical staffing. From 1984, a separate health authority project working on preschool preventive speech therapy was attached to the Riverside project. The core team remained otherwise much the same until late 1985–mid 1986.

The Riverside project's activities have been diverse, reflecting the original aims in a variety of ways. The project team has provided all the medical input to local child health clinics and schools — initially and until 1985 at a level higher than the city average. This meant, for example, that doctors were committed to visit schools weekly or fortnightly throughout the school year, and that two doctors would staff child health clinics, both to provide training opportunities and to allow informal discussion with parents outside the consulting room. Post-clinic discussion of all children seen with the clinic staff has enabled the team, including the family health visitor, to spot any relevant problems or areas for action.

Each member of the project team has had a unique contribution to make. The health visitor's role has been heterogeneous, involving her in most areas of the project's activity. She continued to hold a limited case load (54 families with children aged 0–5 years and 46 elderly families). With this group she carried out the normal range of health visiting duties. She worked with parent groups, on one-off, short-term and long-term bases. For example, in the early days of the Riverside project she worked with a local midwife to organise an antenatal group in a local community centre. This group lasted about 12 months, with a varying population, including some post-natal mums who continued to attend. It covered an immense range of subjects, far more than either professional had expected, and many of which were not usually included in classes. Caesareans, epidurals, post-natal depression and episiotomies were some of the areas which came up again and again. Both of the professionals learnt a lot about working with groups from this experience, because things definitely did not run smoothly! In a local playgroup, the Riverside project health visitor became involved in the local management committee, dealing with budget and staffing concerns, as well as dropping in on the group on a regular basis and being used as a resource, informally or in specific sessions. She also contributed to various groups on a 'one-off or two-off' basis on topics such as first aid, what health visitors do and contraception. In all of the groups enabling parents to share their knowledge and skills was crucial.

Another area of the project health visitor's work was liaison with colleagues — in health visiting and school nursing and also in management. She has also been involved in representing a health visiting view in discussions within the team itself. Because of the service commitment of the team and the implications for developing responsive services, the project health visitor also became involved in research and development in the area — evaluating services, looking at clients' views of services, and developing new patterns of practice in conjunction with colleagues. The other main area of her work has been in training: as an individual in discussion with students, through involvement in the planning and presentation of weekly discussion meetings for professionals, and in more formal presentations of the project's work or courses organised by the project.

The Riverside project has tried out different ways of working in nurseries and schools, involving parents, teachers, health visitors, doctors, community workers, school nurses, educational psychologists and education welfare officers, among others. In nurseries, health visitors have worked with parents, teachers and doctors to identify children in whom possible health needs existed, and to take appropriate action (Pearson, 1985a). At school entry health visitors have been encouraged to use a formalised handover of information to school health staff about children who they feel may require additional support or help.

In school, parents have been involved from before the entry of their children with information about the school health service and the system of class reviews operated (Table 1). This review system has freed school health staff from routine medicals and given them not only better communication with other professionals working with children, but also time to develop work with parents and children, for example on asthma (Colver, 1984). Project community workers have spent time with groups of parents in schools and nurseries, and have helped and encouraged other team members in work with parents in these settings.

Information-sharing, both between professionals, as in the examples above, and between parents and professionals, has been an important part of the Riverside project's work. Although more obviously a part of the community work, it has also strongly influenced patterns of practice by health professionals. As well as the deliberate and central involvement of parents in nursery and class reviews (and the

Table 1   *Procedure of Entry Class Reviews*

Term	Action
Summer term/ autumn term	Parents' meetings; booklets issued explaining school health service. Doctor and nurse attend and talk informally. Health visitors hand over in person to school nursing sisters details of children who they think may have problems in school
Autumn term	Hearing and vision tests are commenced on new entrants after half-term. Children identified at hand-over are followed up as appropriate.

Spring term	Letters sent to parents asking them to identify any concerns about their child to nurse, doctor or head.
	    Review meetings are arranged for head and class teachers, school nursing sister, school doctor and others as relevant, e.g. educational psychologist, education social worker. Each meeting lasts about 1 hour. The outcome may be
	
	1 No action
	2 Ongoing action (already initiated)
	3 New action: medical
	                         nursing
	                         other

Spring term/ summer term	Selective medical examinations. Nursing reviews and assessments. Group work with children/parents. Special campaigns, e.g. asthma.

attempt to involve parents in the way these work), attitudes towards records and the use of parent-held records have been explored (Pearson, 1985b). Parents' views on services have been channelled to the appropriate people, and have resulted in changes, for example in the immunisation appointment system (from monthly to weekly to reduce waiting time), and the provision of facilities for toddlers in the local hospital's antenatal clinic.

Group work has involved both established groups and newly formed ones. Some groups have taken place in schools, nurseries, play groups or people's homes. Others have brought people in to the project's centre — a drop-in centre where leaflets, books, coffee, tea, toys and comfortable chairs are always available. Some groups have a short life span, for example, six sessions spent thinking about relationships. Others are more open-ended, changing their membership over time but interested in a wide range of issues relating to health.

All of the project team have at some time participated in these groups as facilitators or resource people. One group in particular, the information group, has utilised both parents and professionals to provide the basic information for leaflets on topics such as bed-wetting, children's infections, or sleep patterns in young children. Through groups, parents have been able to share experiences with each other and to develop confidence in themselves both as parents and as people. This has been enhanced when professionals have shared not only their information but their uncertainties, and become, however slightly, powerless and thus more human.

Weekly discussion meetings have also been arranged, to which all professionals working with children in the area are invited. These have provided an opportunity for the professionals to get to know each other better and explore each other's roles. Discussion topics have ranged widely, from rashes in children, through speech and language problems to the role of social workers, and unemployment and health.

Students on placement, both short- and long-term, have included students of medicine, social work, nursing, speech therapy and theology. They have not only received from but also contributed to the project, through their questions, from new perspectives, and by their activities, in undertaking studies, working with groups and participating in practice. Many other students and practitioners, including many health visitors, have shared ideas during shorter visits.

Professionals and parents have been involved in the management of the community work part of the Riverside project, learning together to develop the skills required, and offering another opportunity to share information. Although primarily directed towards community work initiatives, feedback from these meetings has sometimes related to health service provision, for example, the amount of information given to parents prior to or following hearing and vision testing in school. It has also had implications for community health — for instance, the availability of healthy food for children in schools, nurseries and leisure facilities in the area.

Each of the project's aims has generated particular types of response from the team, but undoubtedly the most important in its influence on the project's activities was the third aim — essentially stating that the project's professionals should enable parents, families and the local community to keep children healthy; to take responsibility for and power over their children's health, to understand the factors which affect it, and to look critically at the services available to help them in maintaining or regaining it. This aim has always been more difficult for the health professionals to get to grips with than for the community workers. It is perhaps one of the strengths of the project that the team has continued to pursue this. It is also a major area of irritation for those who feel that services are already responsive, that parents are given sufficient information about their children's health by professionals, and that, particularly in a disadvantaged area, professionals can assess health needs more effectively than parents — in other words, that the status quo is satisfactory.

One key to many of the problems experienced by health professionals and others with the third aim is power. Health professionals have been educated to see themselves as advisers, counsellors and experts, and are often seen by parents in those roles (Pearson, 1984). Parents want — and need — reassurance about their decisions on matters of health and illness. Ultimately however, as every health visitor knows, it is the parents who make the decisions; to have the immunisation or not; to change their meals or not;

to use health services or not. Professional power lies in maintaining control of the information necessary to make some or all of these decisions. There is a subtle but important distinction between providing accurate and appropriate information, on the basis of which health decisions can be made by the client, and advising the client as to appropriate action. It is is of course still possible for the client to take alternative action, but it requires self-confidence, and confidence in alternative information. All information is presented within a value framework. The information which the client already possesses — from experience, or other sources — is also part of a value framework. This may be the same as or different from the other, adding a further complication to the apparently simple task of informing parents about health and health services. A further difficulty, which periodically caused problems for team members, is that much of the information usually looked at relates to individual solutions to problems, yet collective or community solutions — political solutions — might be more appropriate.

Sharing of both information and power has been the central feature of the work of the Riverside project. A diverse team of professionals has shared an office, and shared their perspectives. Parents and professionals — with and without community work skills — have shared information, and contributed to each other's decision-making.

What are the particular lessons of the Riverside project for health visitors? First of all the importance for service providers of looking at the health needs of their local community. Secondly, the importance of doing this in conjunction with other professionals, whose perspectives will offer a broader, fuller picture, and with clients, who after all are experiencing the needs. The third lesson is that identifying need is not enough. The services provided must be evaluated, not only by professionals, but also by clients, who can say what is missing and what is important to them. The service must then be developed appropriately.

Particularly in the area of child health, there has been a tendency for services to retain relatively traditional principles and procedures. Riverside project has begun to look at new ways of working, following up ideas and discarding those which were unsuccessful. Perhaps the fourth lesson is this: to question the status quo, and examine it critically, to support it when it is appropriate, and to develop new approaches and ways of working when it is not. When this is not just part of a project, but part of every health visitor's way of working, we shall be moving towards providing a more effective and responsive service. Where teaching or training is part of our job, we will benefit particularly from the fresh insights and creative ideas of newcomers.

Teamwork, with clients/consumers/lay people and with other professionals, is the key to effective community health work. Riverside project demonstrated one model whereby a variety of health professionals were brought into closer contact with the people of their local community. Thus they were enabled, through community work — both directly and indirectly in its influence on their views and philosophy — to work more effectively and responsively for that community.

CASE STUDY 7

IMPROVING HEALTH CARE FOR THE HOMELESS

Anne Cross

When homeless families were first placed in bed and breakfast accommodation, the provision of primary health care was not considered a problem. The health visitors concerned carried out their visits without any special preparation or training. Most referrals were received in the normal manner from the post-natal wards. The only indication that these families were any different from other clients was the addresses of the hotels, often with exotic names such as Marco Polo, New Dawn and Albatross. But as the number of families steady rose and the length of stay also increased, health visitors were forced to consider the problem in greater depth.

At one time families presenting at local authority housing departments without accommodation were split up, with the parents being sent to hostels and the children placed in care. After the 1977 Housing (Homeless Persons) Act, the local authorities were required to secure accommodation for those in priority need. This led to a search for temporary accommodation because of insufficient local authority housing. As the funds available for building low-cost housing diminished, local authority housing stock was sold off and moderate-rent accommodation in the private sector became scarce, the availability of suitable low-cost housing continued to decline. The steady increase in the number of homeless families with children under 5 years of age in London and particularly in the Bayswater area can be seen in Fig. 2. In addition there are the so-called intentionally homeless, who, according to the 1977 Housing Act, do not qualify for council accommodation and who have nowhere else to live other than in the hostels which abound in this district of London.

In the light of the growing volume of work caused by larger case loads and the unusual demands of homeless families, health visitors in this area of London began to

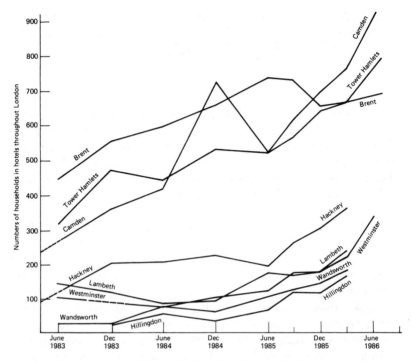

Fig. 2 Total number of households placed in hotels by selected London boroughs from June 1983. From GLC Housing Research and Policy Report no. 4; Shelter and Bayswater Project surveys. Westminister: figure for December 1983 is unknown

question the effectiveness of their visits. One of the first indications that new methods of work had to be considered was the attitude of the families to the initial visit. Health visitors could easily be confused with local authority personnel who had placed the family in the hotel. The health visitor was quickly seen as the person to right all wrongs. This led to the dilemma that the advice being sought was often of a complexity that no ordinary health visitor could be expected to know. And yet not to discuss the immediate problem, housing rights, would be insensitive to say the least and certainly not conducive to establishing a working relationship. This situation was a recipe for frustration for both client and worker. As time passed, a body of information was built up which enabled the health visitor to act as a link person and to be seen as a credible source of relevant information. It was only then that the health visitor was able to offer health advice and education which was likely to be accepted.

HEALTH PROBLEMS OF THE HOMELESS

Having recognised the priority need of the homeless, and embarked on the delivery of health care, the health problems were more easily identified and more daunting. These were as follows.

Nutrition

Practical advice had to be based on the fact that cooking facilities were either non-existent or shared in distant basements between a dozen or so families. Lack of money in an area (Bayswater) which is unusually expensive had to be considered. Another factor was the absence of available space in hotel rooms which could encourage eating in a disciplined way and so lead to good eating habits.

Safety

The prevention of accidents in hazardous surroundings, which included steep stairways often without banisters, access to dangerous roof areas and little or no protection from electrical appliances such as kettles and irons, requires high levels of imaginative and convincing advice.

Infections

Unhygienic conditions and overcrowding exacerbated the problem of infectious diseases. Diseases such as gastroenteritis, infectious skin conditions and communicable diseases were quickly passed from family to family.

Other areas which presented problems of adequate health care services were antenatal care, completion of immunisation programmes, dental treatment, family planning services and appropriate care and advice for families experiencing problems associated with child abuse.

Developmental delay was also frequently observed. Children were often strapped into pushchairs or kept in cots for excessive periods of time in order to protect them from danger in small overcrowded rooms, with the result that normal physical development such as walking and crawling could be slow. Speech and language delays were associated with parents too depressed to provide the necessary stimulation for their babies to learn.

Stress between parents resulted in anxiety in their children which sometimes manifested itself in behavioural disorders. Wilson and Jenkins (1985) have described this in their research:

> Parents were asked if they were worried about the behaviour of their children. The three most common problems were fussing about meals, eating properly and daily temper tantrums. Sleep disturbances were also common. Of the 36 children over the age of 1 year for whom information was available, 12 had possible behavioural problems.

Health visitors, faced with the overwhelming and complex problem of providing health care to the families, began to explore the possibility of alternative methods of work. To continue with the traditional approach was not only inadequate for the clients, it was also demoralising for the workers. It was becoming clear that whatever the changes that might be introduced, a special support network should be included in the scheme. The stress experienced by workers in this field was considerable.

ACTION

It was clear that health visitors working with homeless families in the hotel setting were in a unique position to identify the needs of this client group. From this experience it was decided to take two courses of action. Firstly, to try to provide a safe and stimulating environment for the children with their parents; this led to the setting up of the parents' and under-5s' group. Secondly, it was agreed to make contact with others working in the same field in order to exchange information which might result in an improved level of service for the homeless; this led to the establishment of the co-ordinating group for the homeless in Bayswater.

The Parents' and Under-5s' Group

The first steps entailed contact with the Pre-School Playgroups' Association which was able to give advice as to what the minimum requirements would be. There were three priorities: money, premises and a constant source of good advice. A group was formed consisting of a community worker from a local voluntary agency, a health visitor and members of the Pre-School Playgroups' Association. In fact, the exploration of the various avenues thought to be of use was helpful in attaining the second objective, contact with local community and other workers.

Funding was a major problem. The time and effort required to secure this was considerable. Personal contact followed by letters followed by personal contact appeared to be the best method. A number of trusts with special interests in children or homelessness were approached, as were the Greater London Council (GLC) Women's Committee and National Appeals. The first grant received was from Capital Radio, the second from the National Council of Children's Voluntary Organisations Under-5s Initiatives. Grants were later received from two local authorities which have homeless families placed in the vicinity. As soon as funding was confirmed a management committee of five officers, including a treasurer, secretary and chairperson, was formed. A simple constitution was drawn up and a bank account opened. A health visitor was a member of the management committee.

The second major problem was finding suitable premises. In a 2-year period the group has had to move no less than five times. Bayswater is an expensive district where property values seem to know no limits. Church organisations have been able to help on a temporary basis and on two occasions the group functioned in NHS property which has been awaiting sale. Contacts within the community have been essential in order to survive. At present, permanent premises are again being sought with the help of church financing and NHS support. Other charities are being approached for further funding of the play leaders.

Originally the group was set up with one play leader. This was soon found to be impractical because of the stressful nature of the work. A second play worker was selected for her ability to work not only with children but also with parents who are often depressed or angry. Part of the play leaders' responsibility included outreach work to help newcomers over that difficult first visit to the group.

A programme was initiated which included three regular sessions each week: one with a social worker, one concerning health care with a health visitor and one on housing rights with an advice worker. Members of the management committee also visited regularly in order to support the staff and to monitor the needs of the group. In this way it was hoped that both staff and families had access to the advice and help they needed.

Evaluation of the Parents' and Under-5s' Group

The positive aspects of this group have been primarily that it is a place where the families can relax in a comfortable atmosphere. It is seen as an escape from the isolation of a small cramped room in an unknown part of London. It has given the children the opportunity to play and learn in a spacious area. It offers access to advice on the day-to-day problems of the homeless. This includes the chance to gain health advice from health visitors on an informal basis. In addition to these practical advantages, it offers a platform for discussion which enables both families and workers to examine the needs of the homeless. Anger at conditions can be channelled into positive campaign work, for example. Physical energy can be directed into swimming or other forms of exercise in conjunction with good dietary practice.

Problems encountered here have been the provision of social work help. The need for regular social work support has been recognised but it is difficult to provide. Voluntary agencies have been helpful but irregular in giving this service. A permanent part-time social worker is now being sought.

Encouraging families to participate in the under-5s' group has not been easy. Apathy and depression have to be dispelled. Also the families do not see themselves as a 'homeless group'. This is no doubt due to the stigma of homelessness. Families try hard to dissociate themselves from this image in order to retain their self-respect. An understanding of this feeling helps to overcome the resistance.

The difficulties in securing premises has led to some incorrect decisions. On one occasion, small premises were thought to be better than no premises at all. This proved not to be so, as the families were just moving from one overcrowded situation to another. Space is a priority need for these families and their children.

Servicing such a group requires considerable time and energy. Health visitors need to monitor the hours spent on such a project carefully in conjunction with the benefits to the health and development of the children and their parents. In the case of the Bayswater project and under-5s' group, the positive response of the families and their children has confirmed the need. However, the numbers attending are small, so that in order to provide this service to more families, more groups are needed rather than enlarging the present group. More than 30 families using it intermittently would not be appropriate.

Co-ordinating Groups for the Homeless in Bayswater

The health visitors made contact with various individuals and community groups working with the homeless. It was agreed that a meeting should be convened inviting all those known to be involved in this work. The following representatives were invited:

> Members of voluntary agencies including Shac, Shelter, Mind, Welcare.
> Local church representatives of several denominations.
> Education welfare personnel.
> Health personnel, including health visitors, clinical medical officer and GPs.
> Social worker from the local area office.
> Secretary of the Community Health Council.
> Members of the local community and homeless families.

It was agreed at this meeting that the agencies should work together and that the first task would be to draft an application to the GLC to establish a new project in Bayswater for the homeless. This would provide advice and gather information in order to increase general awareness of the problem of homelessness. The co-ordinating group would meet every 6 weeks to exchange information and monitor the progress of the Bayswater project. In this way the project would be able to respond to the needs of the homeless.

Funding for the project was originally provided by the GLC and Shelter, with grants from local authorities who place families in the Bayswater area. Subsequently, an EEC grant was obtained. The Bayswater project comprises four workers, two advice persons, one administrator and research person. One member of staff speaks Bengali.

The co-ordinating group has expanded. It now includes school principals, a Committee for Racial Equality representative, members of other local advice agencies, to name but a few. A newsletter and statistical information are sent to all those on the mailing list. In order to improve communications various personnel from local authorities placing families in Bayswater have been invited to the meetings. These include directors of housing or homeless person's units, directors of social services, educational personnel, members of local social security departments as well as elected representatives. The exchange of information has been useful and lively.

The formation of the under-5s' group and the co-ordinating group has had a positive effect on both workers and clients. Clients now have easier access to professional advice based on local circumstances. Some of the services are more easily co-ordinated, although much more could be done in this area. Health visitors have been released from responsibilities of giving housing advice which allows more time for delivering health care and health information. Environmental health problems are dealt with by the project; this enables families to point out hazardous aspects of the hotels without jeopardising their relationship with the managers.

The Bayswater project has carried out campaign activities which have brought to the attention of those in authority the needs of the homeless in Bayswater. Some changes have taken place and more are planned.

Evaluation of Additional Services

The achievements of the last 5 years have been difficult to assess because of the relentless increase in the number of families being accommodated temporarily in bed and breakfast hotels. Extra child health sessions, doubling the number of clinical medical officers at these sessions, the introduction of a full-time Bengali interpeter for four sessions weekly, and the increase in family planning clinics have all been welcomed. However, all additional services have been unable to keep up with the growth in the volume of work. In fact as progress has been made in improving referral systems and as communication with non-English speaking families has improved, the enormity of the health problems has become more apparant and pressing.

As workers have become more aware of these health needs, a body of information has been built up which can be used not only in Bayswater but throughout the country where similar problems exist. The experience of working with other disciplines has proved invaluable. It has enabled health visitors to obtain support from their colleagues in other disciplines to convince management of the need for change. Independent bodies such as the Community Health Council, local pressure groups and national campaign organisations have also contributed to the push for change in services.

FUTURE PLANS

The modest successes have given rise to high expectations for the future. Better methods of delivery of health care must be found. Acknowledgement of a problem highlighted by the media, members of the community and co-workers has led to the reassessment of this provision. In the case of the Bayswater homeless, suggestions from the health workers and others have included the formation of a care team for the homeless comprising a multi-disciplinary group which includes members of the voluntary sector. Suggested members of the care team for the homeless are:

> Health visitors and supporting staff
> GPs or clinical medical officers
> Interpreter
> Social worker
> Advice worker
> Play worker
> Midwives for the antenatal sessions
> Educational welfare officers
> (Some of these would be full-time workers, others would work on a sessional basis)

The advantages would be better channels of communication, the formation of appropriate support networks for the workers and a more cost-effective method. Access to advice and help for the families would be in a more convivial atmosphere, since play facilities would be one of the services available.

Finally, this approach would allow health visitors the opportunity of reassessing their professional standards in the context of providing the health care which is most appropriate to the needs of these families in crisis.

CONCLUSIONS

Observation of the changing needs of the community, in this case the increasing number of homeless in Bayswater, has forced health visitors to see the problem in a wider context. The obvious solution for these hotel families is the provision of an adequate supply of decent, low-cost housing so that temporary accommodation is not required. The families would then be able to face their individual problems and all the normal stresses and strains of family life without the additional disadvantage of hotel existence.

However, this leaves the health visitor with the present dilemma. It is a challenge which has been partially met. Imaginative health programmes can be initiated, but this needs not only extra resources but a better understanding of the problem and encouragement from both management and colleagues in order to succeed.

4
Using Groups to Develop Health Visiting Practice

The previous two chapters have looked at how health visitors use groups to enhance their practice for their clients. This chapter examines how health visitors use groups for themselves. Much is written about the need for support for health visitors but very little is written about the practical details of how this might happen. The following three case studies give detailed accounts of how health visitors have come together to create an atmosphere of support and effect change. Each depicts very different initiatives. Rowe relates the development of a peer support group. Pittaway *et al.* describe the creation of district-wide workshops, while Spray recounts the growth of a national network. The first two case studies describe responses by health visitors to their work situations within the framework of their work while the last describes a response outside the work environment.

All of the activities in these case studies arose out of a recognition of the needs of health visitors. Rowe describes the feelings of isolation experienced by health visitors. Pittaway *et al.* highlight the sensation of powerlessness felt by many health visitors facing families living in situations of multiple deprivations. Spray outlines the frustrations experienced by health visitors as a socially and politically educated group of nurses in the NHS. The case studies relate positive action taken to begin dealing with the experience of health visiting. The main thrust of each case study is that health visitors were brought together in groups to share their feelings and experiences. The health visitors were then able to act together in finding solutions.

A main theme in each case study is that of the development of support for health visitors. The support described is professional yet personal at the same time. Pittaway *et al.* relate how health visitors can be collectively empowered to find solutions to problems that can seem overwhelming to individuals. Spray writes of the confidence that can develop in individuals from sharing ideas and knowledge. Rowe describes the strength that can come from having opportunities to look at problems objectively with colleagues.

One striking aspect of all the case studies is how creative it is for health visiting practice to set aside time for health visitors to meet together to discuss their work. Each author underlines the richness of debate that is created by combining forces, whether to do with health visiting advice or with issues that impinge on health visiting practice. Too often debate centres on issues that are rarely raised, but these case studies show the need to discuss aspects such as racism in health visiting. By creating opportunities for health visitors collectively to examine and question their rationale and methods, a wealth of imaginative and positive ideas for practice are developed. Pittaway *et al.* describe the range of initiatives, from a health visitor-initiated consultative group for management to new health education materials, that resulted from their workshops.

An important aspect of each case study is that separate time was created for health visitors to be together to discuss their work. Rowe writes of fortnightly meetings, Pittaway *et al.* describe day-long workshops for all health visitors employed in their health district, while Spray writes of weekend workshops. Pittaway *et al.* viewed this as getting off the treadmill and stepping back from work to view it more objectively. Rowe emphasises that through the process of the support group meetings the health visitors became more analytical of their work.

By creating the time to step back from work and critically examine practice — whether concerning individual handling of a particular interaction with a family or district-wide

or nationally — is of immeasurable value to the entire
health visiting community. Health visitors gain strength
and confidence from talking with each other. They are also
able to critically evaluate their work as well as the issues that
impinge on them, and then develop new solutions.

CASE STUDY 8

HEALTH VISITORS TALKING

Jean Rowe

The first year of health visiting was an unhappy and bewildering time for me. Apart from the traumas of grappling with a totally new work setting, the clinic itself was staffed by a seething mass of angry women who had retreated into secretive unfriendly behaviour not only towards one another but also towards us — us being another new health visitor and myself. We had been students together. She was the only person I was able to confide in and I think that helped us both to cope. When we most needed a guiding hand and the wisdom of experience, it was never willingly offered. Even the extremely efficient clinic clerk had a cold silent air about her. She filled in the birth book, did the filing, transferred records in and out, made lists for developmental checks and immunisations and sent out appointments. What a gem she was, but I never did find out how she did all these things. I just took it all for granted. We were told to go out visiting by 10 o'clock and be back at 4, but we could come in at lunch-time. A very important part of my education was missing and I felt too afraid to ask why and how things were done.

The health visitors' office had six desks all turned towards the wall. We even had our coffee made for us — the clerk did this too. In retrospect, it was an administratively well organised clinic. It had to be since nobody really communicated with one another. The organisation ran like a machine but it was totally inhuman. The other new health visitor and I worked very hard indeed. The feelings of guilt were enormous if the visiting quota was not achieved, but at least the families were human and welcoming.

So who was health visiting whom? Nobody told us to slow down, that time can be a resource, when families can work on solutions to their problems, and that the health visitor is more often the listener and rarely the 'doer'. The frenetic activity produced feelings of worthlessness, frustration and gloom. Guilt-ridden, I started to sit in the cemetery when I could not face yet another new face. There at least I knew I could not be found. Needless to say I left health visiting after the requisite year and so did my friend. The last straw was my attempt to apply for a travelling scholarship to carry out a weaning study. The training officer accepted my proposal with great interest but permission to go ahead with the application was refused by the senior nursing officer.

There is a basic contradiction and dilemma here. We cannot support anyone else if we do not receive support ourselves. That is not selfishness but reality. We are human first and health visitors second. We have the same emotions as the clients we serve. Does health visiting mean that we can only express feelings when at home and act as another person when at work? The pent-up anger we sometimes feel can have drastic consequences for us if we are not allowed to express emotions like a normal person.

Health visitors do support one another but only in a conducive and friendly setting. We do not always like the people we have to work with and in the health service we can rarely choose our work place either. If we do not like the people we work with, it does not necessarily mean that we cannot work together. A sense of trust plus respect for other people can enhance a working relationship.

I believe that health visitors can support one another without the help of an expert facilitating the process. That is not to say that other types of interaction groups are not appropriate. They are, and can be used for differing and personal learning needs. Having participated in several interdisciplinary groups over the last 2 years prior to setting up a health visitor group, members of other community caring services were appalled that health visitors did not consult with or receive counselling by their seniors when dealing with difficult family situations. It may be that health visitors feel they ought to be able to cope and are failing if they cannot. In the absence of other types of support, a health visitor-run support group might raise awareness of the possibilities of differing types of support. It is helpful but not essential if at least one health visitor has had some experience of leading or participating in a group. Outside help is often not available when it is most needed.

We decided to run a pilot group in the clinic. The idea arose from a study done by the Institute of Marital Studies in our health district where for more than 2 years psychotherapists sat in the group while we presented family studies. We found that we had become better listeners and the health visitors were becoming more analytical about their client interventions. In some cases we had to admit that the feelings and emotions we felt when dealing with some clients were a reflection of the client's emotional state and that it was quite normal to feel that way. It was not a failing but a positive sensitive reaction. There were always situations when grey areas in family intervention led to discussion about whether to refer the family to another agency or whether it was appropriate to 'hold' for a while to see how the situation developed. Some problems in the families were so deep-rooted and multi-faceted that we had to realise that our energies would be better spent lending support to community action since roots lay in a social and political framework.

Since we had staff meetings for the sector every fortnight, we thought that a clinic-based group might be feasible on the alternate weeks. Initially we decided that we should meet in the lunch hour but since we would be talking about our work, why not say that we required an hour a fortnight to meet? We put our request in writing to our nursing officer with a copy to the director of nursing services (community), stating that we wished to run a pilot series. We also affirmed that where necessary the nursing officer would be invited if clinic management was an issue for discussion, but that initially the meeting would only be for the health visitors. It was felt that the health visitors would feel more able to talk if the nursing officer was not present since issues of coping or not coping might be construed as a personal weakness. While this may not be so, it was essential to create a safe place to talk. Permission was granted and we went ahead.

The pilot group started on a fortnightly basis for a series of six meetings. At the first meeting we had to agree on a few ground rules. Those who wished to attend had to commit themselves to an hour a fortnight. They should notify the group beforehand if they were unable to attend and explain why. We did not wish people to drift in and out of the group and cause disruption. To a certain extent the content of the meetings was left open so that anyone who felt an urgent need to discuss a pressing problem could be accommodated.

At first the group tended to discuss families with multiple and often intractable problems. This highlighted the frustrating nature of intervention with families in crisis but it did help people identify help that could be offered by other agencies or to see that all that could be achieved on a health visiting level was being done. We talked about areas of clinical practice in an attempt to minimise the problem of giving conflicting advice to clients. Often one person would take the responsibility of opening a discussion by presenting some information. It was amazing how many ideas came out of these discussions with the differing rationales behind the giving of advice. Subjects for discussion included weaning practices, immunisation, advertising by the milk companies, personal feelings about working in the clinic, myths and fantasies that we have about one another and what it was like to be a newcomer to the health visiting team.

We evaluated the first series, acknowledging that if group members felt that it had been a waste of their time they should be able to say so. The consensus was that the group had been very useful and valuable. In fact our first group had run with few hiccups. A second series was suggested which would meet monthly instead of fortnightly. However within the first month health visitors kept asking when the next meeting would be as they had something they really wished to talk about. The group agreed to fortnightly meetings again and the dates were set. We also decided to have a rotating convenor so that each person would have the opportunity of being the group facilitator. This was necessary not only from an organisational point of view but also because at times the group tended to dissolve into a 'cocktail party' chatter session where a lot of talking was going on with very little listening. The convenor's job was to intervene and draw the group back to the topic being discussed. This digressing appeared to happen particularly when rumours of change were circulating in the district, or when there were to be realignments in staffing arrangements. This always caused a lot of anxiety since it not only meant yet another work load upheaval for some people, but a grieving process induced by the loss of a colleague.

Each series was different with a unique personality of its own. Some were more successful than others in a professional and personal sense. On some occasions some health visitors were going through personal and family traumas and needed to voice their anxieties. This was a difficult area as the group can focus on individual needs at the expense of others' needs. The effect of this was almost to destroy the group. The situation had to be carefully handled in order to keep to the agreed group criteria. On reflection, the group may have already fulfilled an earlier expressed need and perhaps should have dissolved in its present form and renegotiated the criteria. The group had been particularly helpful to newly trained health visitors and they were reluctant for it to stop. Perhaps a new type of group could have been formed to suit their unique needs. It was evident that people were communicating much better on a day-to-day basis, especially when dealing with situations that were frustrating and difficult. There was certainly much less tension between the health visitor and the rest of the clinic staff. Before the group was set up myths and fantasies had abounded about each other and how we coped with the job.

Since this experience of participating in group activity, I have become very aware of the potential of working in groups. They can be fun, very creative and bring a sense of belonging. Far from wasting time, which was a worry expressed by some of the health visitors when we originally decided to try peer support, the amount of knowledge, information and ideas that emerged surprised us all. People are resources for other people and, as a result of the group, each health visitor became a resource for the community. When requests were made to the clinic for a health visiting input, we were able to identify which health visitor had the interest and expertise available for the community group need.

It was surprisingly easy to set up the group since most people felt they could commit 1 hour a fortnight. It certainly became a focal point for health visitors based on GPs' surgeries, who welcomed this contact with their colleagues. Part-time health visitors also found it useful since they sometimes felt they missed out and needed the contact. Apart from the social contact, communication improved all round, with a better understanding of our strengths and weaknesses.

To be aware of current trends and explore new ideas, feel involved in a clinic team and recognise the value of health visiting for the consumers, we should all be talking to one another and reviewing our practice. We cannot do this alone but we can do it together.

CASE STUDY 9

HEALTH VISITOR WORKSHOPS: A METHOD FOR SUPPORT

Carol Pittaway, Carol Sinker and Anne Wood

While many depriving factors relevant to child and adult health are to be found in large cities throughout Britain, certain districts such as Tower Hamlets in London appear to have a combination of problems that create enormous pressure on the NHS, particularly in the area of primary care. These problems are compounded by the poor social, economic and environmental conditions that exist within the district. A profile of health and social morbidity reveals a population which is in the main disadvantaged and vulnerable, requiring from its health professions a flexible and innovative approach to health care provisions in order to meet the needs of such a diverse population.

The issue of how health visitors can overcome their sense of powerlessness and frustration in differing situations was explored in two workshops. These workshops enabled health visitors to start to become more able to look at their own working difficulties in a constructive way, rather than focussing specifically on problems within the community.

The health visitors involved in this way of working believe it to be not only a way of acknowledging that a problem exists but also taking steps towards resolving it. They have recognised the importance of group support in empowering staff to combat the paralysis of mind and spirit that so often accompanies working in areas overloaded with stress factors.

The most important factors in what has taken place have been the willingness of field workers to take the initiative in seeking solutions, and willingness on the part of management to give credence to what staff are saying, enabling them to take time out to develop new strategies that will empower not only themselves, but also the families with whom they work in the community.

WORKSHOP 1:   A FRESH LOOK AT HEALTH VISITING WITH THE BANGLADESHI COMMUNITY

Historically the Spitalfields and Whitechapel areas of Tower Hamlets borough have been a haven for new immigrants. The most recent arrivals have come from Sylhet, a rural district in north-east Bangladesh. The move began in the 1950s and gathered momentum; currently areas of Tower Hamlets have a very high concentration of Bangladeshi families. These families in many instances live in the most profound state of deprivation in terms of poverty, low-quality housing, and poor environment.

These factors, linked with language barriers and multiple health needs, created what seemed to be insurmountable problems for health visitors who had 70–100% non-English speaking case loads. Within the support groups which existed at that time, the health visitors shared with a senior clinical psychologist (community) their great dissatisfaction with the services they were offering these families. With her encouragement management were approached to seek ways of changing the situation. Management agreed to the idea of staff taking time out to look at the problems and find a solution, if possible.

In April 1984 a working party was set up, comprising health visitors, a senior clinical psychologist and a senior nurse specialist. The multi-disciplinary mix was an effective exercise in team work, and showed a total openness between field staff and management. Following the formation of the working party it was decided that, as it was a workshop for health visitors, those health visitors involved should be consulted about who should attend, in what capacity, and what should be included in the workshop.

All health visitors who met the criteria of >70% Bengali case loads attended a planning workshop meeting. Following this meeting it was decided:

1   To allow the working party to develop the programme in consultation with staff.
2   To include a small number of speakers from the Bangladeshi community.

3   To include managers in the workshops.
4   To arrange clinic cover in the absence of staff.
5   To investigate work done by other health visitors in large immigrant communities.
6   To provide participants with local community reports for comment.

Spending time and money looking at one's own work and difficulties exposed health visitors to the charge of egocentrism. Despite this possible criticism they pursued the development of the workshop convinced that unless solutions were found to their sense of powerlessness and frustrations an innovative approach to their work would never emerge. The senior clinical psychologist provided a vital role in supporting the planning group and enabling them to feel able to make changes despite constant anxieties about either lifting the lid off an insurmountable problem, or total apathy at the workshop.

It was seen to be important to step outside the working area in order to explore new ways of working, and so the workshop was held in the King's Fund Centre in Camden, on 20 and 21 August 1984. The actual running of the workshop benefited enormously from the help provided by a project worker for the King's Fund and the real sense of keenness and participation of field staff and managers.

The workshop was basically divided into two sections:

1   Acknowledging there was a problem and defining needs (day 1).
2   Seeking ways to meet the defined needs (day 2).

There were sessions of information given by Bangladeshi people and by video, discussions and small group workshops.

The small group workshop entitled 'What are we worrying about?' allowed small groups to talk through what we were most concerned about. For example, how much were western norms and ideas being imposed on an Asian population? The expectations of clients and management as to the standard and style of service that should be offered were felt to be quite different, particularly regarding the Bangladeshis' quite legitimate preoccupation with housing problems, over which health visitors (and apparently the housing departments) have little influence. Those health issues which health visitors can influence take second place to the problems of housing and poverty. This inability to solve what are fundamental economic and political problems brings on a feeling of impotence and powerlessness in the individual health visitor. Finally, a major concern expressed was that of 'not being Bangladeshi' and the need for more Bangladeshi people to become involved in the health care system.

The two small group workshops entitled 'Are the health needs different from other immigrants or the indigenous population?' and 'Is it more than a language problem?' helped us to look at our concerns in an objective way. The conclusions reached were firstly, that the Bengali cultural belief about the body and health and their knowledge and appreciation of the workings of the human body play an important part in the community's concept of what health is. Secondly, specific stresses are placed on a health visitor with a high Bangladeshi case load, for example, difficulty in communication without a common language, difficulty in building up a relationship through a third party, ignorance of cultural and religious practices and myths and the demand on our time by the client's hospitality (indeed a great deal of meaningful health visiting seems to be done as one is heading for the door at the end of the visit). However many of the problems encountered were no different to those encountered by health visitors with an indigenous case load. The main difference is that the number of problems is usually greater per family and per case load.

One other big concern expressed was that of racism — both within ourselves and encountered in others.

Irritation with management requirements and service limitations also came to the surface in these sessions. Inadequate in-service education about the Bangladeshi community and lack of health education material specific to their needs was another source of frustration.

Two other small groups discussed ways of adapting health visiting practice. Identified needs included:

1 Training and development of all health workers.
2 Support for staff and clients.
3 A consultative process developed with field staff managers.
4 Closer liaison with management concerning health visiting and ethnic minorities.
5 Encouraging self-reliance in clients.
6 Formation of links with the Bengali community and community workers.

The Follow-up

A further half-day meeting was held at King's Fund on 12 September 1984 at which two areas for further work were identified:

1 Client-centred groups, i.e. groups organised by or for clients, in which health visitors are involved.
2 Training of workers both on the role of the health visitor and on the customs and beliefs of the Bangladeshi culture.

A workshop steering group was elected to organise a follow-up day, and generally to maintain an overall view of how projects were developing.

Since that workshop there have been a number of outcomes. Health visitors have met regularly for a period of time to share their experiences in various client-centred groups. An education group has been set up to look at developing an ethnic minority resource centre. Health visitors have become involved in a local community maternity health workers' scheme, which has allowed shared work and training to be carried out. New health education material has been developed. Links have been formed with other agencies to address some of the most severe housing issues. Finally, the health visitor-initiated consultative group with management is now well established.

WORKSHOP 2: CLIMBING OFF THE TREADMILL

In response to low morale and a feeling of being on the treadmill in the health visiting unit of East Tower Hamlets, the senior nurse (training) suggested holding a similar 2-day workshop in May 1985. A steering group was formed to facilitate planning and organisation. This group consisted of four health visitors, the senior nurse (training) and the senior clinical psychologist.

The steering group met on 10 occasions. We were constantly aware of the need to represent the needs and aspirations of all potential participants in the planning process. Consultation was therefore an important part of the group work, enabling everyone to feel part of the final product.

The group isolated five problems relating to health visiting practice. These were presented as questions in order to stimulate easier discussion at the workshop.

1 Families with multiple problems — Is there a solution?
2 Child health clinics — What is the right approach?
3 Group work — Is it the way forward?
4 Home visiting — Is it effective?
5 Working with other professionals — Myth or reality?

A later addition to the list of questions was the issue of support and appraisal. We felt it was significant that our feeling of lack of support had not been isolated earlier as a contributing cause to our concern about the other issues.

Again, it seemed important that our workshop should be held away from Tower Hamlets. Arrangements were made to use the regional training centre at Oaklea, in the Essex countryside, and residential accommodation was available. It proved an ideal setting, with the majority of health visitors attending on a residential basis.

Although the workshop was primarily an in-house affair the group felt that working with community groups was an important issue for discussion, and so an outside speaker, Vari Drennan, was invited to discuss this particular development in health visiting practice.

Another issue for discussion was the appropriateness or otherwise of management participation. Following consultation with one manager, it was agreed that she and the director of nursing services would attend on the second day. This arrangement proved very valuable in that it allowed participants to feel unrestrained in their contributions on day 1, and allowed the generalised strength of feeling to be conveyed directly to managers on day 2. There was also great value in managers being part of the strategies promoted to overcome problems.

The Workshop

Cover for clinics and emergency cover for crisis situations was arranged, thus allowing a maximum number of health visitors to attend. Clients were informed of the arrangements so there would be minimal disruption. The steering group envisaged day 1 as a cathartic experience, with everyone off-loading, and day 2 providing constructive ideas, leading to positive outcomes. Both as a steering group and as individuals, high levels of anxiety were experienced before the workshop about the belief that the presumptions of the team would dominate and that it was possible that a can of worms might be opened for which there was no workable solution. Worries were dispelled when the 2 days proved to be an extremely exhilarating, emotionally uplifting albeit exhausting experience. Only half the topics suggested were covered, and sessions were never long enough for the ensuing discussion. Our most difficult problem was bringing sessions to a close.

The following areas of concern requiring action were highlighted:

1 Clerical assistance.
2 Working in teams.
3 Record-keeping and the health visiting process.
4 24-hour service and flexitime.
5 Information needs.
6 Care of the elderly.
7 Community hospital liaison.
8 Home visiting.
9 Child health clinics.
10 Group work.
11 The need for support, counselling, appraisal and career guidance.
12 Working with other professionals.
13 The role and status of health visitors.

The workshop decided there were various ways in which we could address these areas of concern. They were:

1 Do nothing.
2 Take local action at clinic or centre level.
3 Form working groups to address specific issues.
4 Take effective action as a large group.

The Follow-up

This half-day session at Oaklea was intended for evaluation and planning action. The breathing space had allowed us to clarify our ideas and evaluate rationally how useful the exercise had been.

Participants had felt the social and psychological aspects of the workshop to be most significant. There was a general feeling of personal empowerment arising out of the collective action of the group. The sense of isolated frustration, once it was shared with colleagues and acknowledged as a legitimate response to working in a stressful environment, disappeared. Instead of being a disparate group scattered throughout the eastern part of Tower Hamlets, we had become united in a spirit of comradeship, which still exists today.

The workshop had freed us to take time out and climb off the treadmill, enabling us as a group to look long and hard at what we were doing and where we were going. This 'space' provided us all with a sense of being enormously refreshed and rejuvenated. The feeling of being unsupported dominated and impinged on many other areas of concern. Deciding what to do about this was difficult but we agreed that sharing it with each other and one manager was a good start.

As a result of the workshop, relationships and communication have improved and we feel increasingly supported by our manager. Staff support groups, facilitated by psychologists, are now running for all health visitors in Tower Hamlets. Finally, working groups have been set up for a number of issues and are making recommendations which will be taken forward by ourselves and management.

CONCLUSIONS

Both workshops have been seen as an exciting and innovative approach by those who participated in them and others who have shared our experience since. Staff were able to take time out and through the process of coming together, sharing and participating in the workshops have felt empowered to seek solutions and initiate change collaboratively with managers and other disciplines.

CASE STUDY 10

THE RADICAL HEALTH VISITORS' GROUP

Jean Spray

The Radical Health Visitors' Group (RHVG) was born out of discontent, as most radical groups are. There is nothing new or unique about a group of health workers being discontented; grumbling is an art form in the NHS and there are many historic and political reasons why it is rarely translated into positive action for change.

In this respect the RHVG broke the mould and it is probably no accident that during the period of the life of the RHVG there was a thriving Radical Nurses' group and a Radical Midwives' group.

It is important to examine the reasons for the formation of the RHVG before examining the important facets of the group, categorised as follows:

1 The difficulties encountered in the struggle for a group identity and confidence.
2 The practical activities and achievements of the group.
3 The impact of the group upon health visitors who were active members.
4 The group's place as a professional and political phenomenon.

Health visitors are seen within the NHS as a socially and politically educated group of nurses; in addition to their nursing and obstetric or midwifery training they are further exposed to a year of sociology, psychology and the social and environmental determinants of illness. Many health visitors believe they are changed by this training but many others adapt the new thinking to the old ways of nursing. Health visitors as a group within the NHS experience the impact of social policies and political decisions on the health and well-being of the community as expressed through housing need, lack of day-care provision and economic poverty. The NHS is unable and unwilling to adopt a collectivist philosophy of health care which would tackle the social causes of health and as a consequence health visitors are a frustrated, isolated and increasingly crisis-ridden group of workers. These frustrations are often expressed when health visitors gather together on courses and seminars and it was at a 1-day research seminar in 1980 that the idea of the RHVG was first raised.

The RHVG never saw itself as a direct challenge to the Health Visitors' Association (HVA): it was not setting out to be an alternative trade union or professional organisation. It saw itself as a ginger group which was prepared to speak out about the profession failing internally to act politically by using the knowledge it had to pressurise political parties and government for social change and failing externally to speak to the world at large by taking a stand on current issues. Multi-national baby food manufacturers and their advertising and promotion policies; nuclear disarmament; feminism and its meaning for health visitors; how to confront racism — these were issues that featured in many of the more successful activities of the RHVG.

The life of the group went through three distinct phases. The initial decision to call a meeting was made by a small group who had attended the research seminar mentioned earlier. There was some limited advertising for the meeting and a significant 'grapevine' effect across London. About 50 people turned up, mainly health visitors. The meeting was confused; there were many bitter complaints about work situations, suspicions about the group being a challenge to the HVA and/or a front for one of the small political parties of the extreme left (it was not). There was no agenda for the meeting and a decision was taken to hold another meeting and discuss why there was a need for such a group.

Several subsequent meetings took place at monthly intervals. These meetings were all held in a polytechnic and resembled a debating group discussing aims and objectives. In addition, regular attenders were getting to know each other.

The next phase of the group was its transition into a politically conscious organisation. This was the longest and most successful period of the group. A small membership fee was established and a regular newsletter produced.

Meetings were advertised in the *Health Visitors' Journal* and other nursing journals. They were held monthly and the venue was a building in central London shared by other pressure groups. There was a small core membership of 6–12 people and this group took on the administration and newsletter production. Sister groups developed in other parts of the country.

During this period a successful leaflet was produced discouraging health visitors from allowing themselves to be used as agents for baby milk and baby food manufacturers by promoting free samples. This leaflet was entitled 'Handing out samples is easy'. Reproduced by photocopy it was extremely popular and sold for a few pence, though many were distributed free.

Organising workshops was the key activity both of the group in the London area, and of those groups in Sheffield, Nottingham and Liverpool. These provided opportunities for up to 50 health visitors to gather together for exchange of news and views. The atmosphere was social and relaxed, usually lasting a whole day and including lunch as well as the sale of books and other campaign literature for many organisations.

The first of these workshops was entitled 'Roots and realities' and studied the often hidden history of health visitors. Other workshops addressed the following topics:

1 Health visitors working in different ways using community development methods.
2 The meaning of nuclear issues for health visitors.
3 Alternatives in health visiting practice.
4 The route to effective political action.
5 Strategies for survival in a changing NHS.

Many individual contributions at these workshops illustrated the growing dilemma faced by many health visitors in their practice. They were increasingly finding that health visiting was leading them into areas defined by managers as political activity. Some examples were:

1 Being involved in a campaign to rid council flats of asbestos by mounting an exhibition in the clinic.

2   Commenting publicly and being reported in the media on the issue of poor nutritional quality of local school meals and subsequently being reprimanded.

The workshops provided a forum for deciding how to raise these issues nationally through the HVA and other organisations which might be sympathetic to these dilemmas. Other pressure groups, such as Child Poverty Action Group, Baby Milk Coalition and War on Want were beginning to take notice of the RHVG and were keen to support ideas and strategies for change.

The monthly meetings in London during this period were well attended and followed a programme of talks and presentations by various members of the group.

One issue which recurred constantly was 'Health visiting — women and feminism'. This also appeared in articles in various issues of the newsletter; when group members were asked to talk to groups of health visitors or student health visitors it was the most frequently requested topic for discussion.

The RHVG appeared with its own banner at the national Campaign for Nuclear Disarmament rally in London in 1982 and later visited the women at Greenham Common to support their action. It could be said that the high point for the RHVG was its contribution to the HVA conference in Brighton in 1982. The group had a stall placed just outside the main exhibition area which attracted a great many conference delegates; many had already heard of the RHVG. Copies of newsletters and leaflets were available.

The HVA was experimenting that year with a new form of platform presentation; this was a pre-prepared debate around the title 'Does political naïvity of health visitors obstruct their ability to influence social change?' A member of the RHVG had been asked to take part in this platform debate, giving her a unique opportunity to air many of the issues which had been hotly debated within the RHVG for the previous 18 months or so. The RHVG also had a successful fringe meeting at the conference on the issue of baby food manufacturers and the free sample racket. This fringe meeting provided a precedent for following years at HVA conferences. The Liverpool group organised a meeting

on race and racism at the 1984 HVA conference and the
Child Poverty Action Group also gained permission to
organise fringe meetings.

Over a period of 4 years the RHVG waxed and waned. Its
strengths were mainly in the efforts of a small consistent
core group whose voluntary time and effort ensured that a
loose but constant network was maintained. The group
never had more than 120 subscribing members but its
sphere of influence was much wider than its membership
numbers. In its final stages in 1984–1985 the small core
group had become exhausted but persisted in organising
monthly meetings in an effort to recruit an alternative core
group. Although many of these meetings were still well
attended it was difficult to interest new people in taking
over the administration and production of the newsletter.
Eventually however new people did take over and the group
survived for several more months.

The RHVG arrived at a crucial period. Political changes
were occurring within the HVA with the appointment of a
new general secretary. The realities of service and financial
cutbacks and the politicisation of health workers was gathering momentum within the NHS. The politics of health
were being widely discussed in the women's movement and
many other pressure groups, in addition to the reawakening
of health as a political issue within the labour and trade
union movement: the RHVG played its part in these
changes. Its strength was that it comprised the workers
themselves. The RHVG had a definite rule from the outset
that only health visitors or student health visitors (although
not necessarily practising) could be members. The group
provided an essential forum for current debate and conflicts
amongst health visitors, many of which have been touched
on in this chapter. It acted as a ginger group for one set of
workers within the NHS — health visitors. It tried to
politicise them and give them strength and support. It
provided a collective sense of shared identity, of increased
confidence; a sense of not being alone and being able to
effect change.

There was a touching but depressing level of political
naïvety in the wider membership, although this tended not

to be true of the core group, members of which had often gained political, organisational and lobbying skills in other places. This is an interesting observation in the light of health visitors' training, which claims to address political processes relating to health and exhorts health visitors to be advocates and community leaders, but political activity within the confines of professional activities is narrowly proscribed.

Many health visitors who attended RHVG workshops and meetings expressed confusion and frustration about the ambiguous messages issued from training colleges and employing authorities over matters involving community activity and action on health.

The RHVG did influence HVA thinking and many health visitors involved in the group were active nationally and locally in the HVA.

In its early days the RHVG produced a working statement:

> The Radical Health Visitors' Group aims to create a personal, social and political awareness among its members. To be called radical, because its members are concerned with developing a fundamental critique of the present practice of health visiting and community health. This would necessarily include consideration of environmental and social as well as personal factors in the promotion and maintenance of health. The group aims to be educational, supportive and active in the future, to pressure for a more appropriate preventative health service.

History is littered with small radical groups which come and go; the RHVG had its place. It was significant. The memory and the lessons should not be lost or forgotten. Many health visitors were touched and influenced by the group and its ideas and activities. I believe they are richer for that experience and in this sense the group was a success.

5

Ideas for Practice

Groups are part of our social existence — families, a circle of friends, belonging to the Women's Institute, a political party, the Health Visitors' Association or a sports club. Health visitors are involved in groups in many different ways and for different reasons. They may be involved as individuals for social reasons, for professional reasons, for support, information or for sharing knowledge and developing ideas. They may be involved on behalf of their clients as a way of supporting them, teaching, sharing knowledge, campaigning or for social change. The case studies in Chapters 2–4 have given excellent examples of how health visitors are involved with groups. This chapter is concerned with some of the practical issues that health visitors need to consider when becoming involved with a group of people and supplements the reality of the experiences related in the case studies.

NETWORKING AND PROFILING

The basis of all good health visiting practice must be a community health profile. Information gathered from informal and formal sources to provide a picture of a community is the key to health visiting, whether with individuals or with groups. A profile should provide information about the experiences of the people in that community as well as demographic and epidemiological statistics. The production of a profile by a group of health visitors serving a geographical area (whether they are GP-attached or geographically based) will not only provide information about health needs but also the basic knowledge health visitors need to share with their clients about services, organisations and structures. Orr (1985) has written in detail about how to compile such a profile. She suggests that 12 topic areas should be covered. These are:

1 Historical.
2 Environmental and spatial characteristics.
3 Organisations.
4 Residents.
5 Social climate.
6 Social and economic features.
7 Power and leadership.
8 Health statistics.
9 Social services.
10 Health services.
11 Health action potential.
12 Health needs.

Health visitors may shudder at the thought of compiling such a profile but many established health visitors have much of this information available anyway but do not have an organised means of sharing it with newer colleagues or students. All students have to provide a profile of an area as part of their training and this exercise could be useful for updating the information. While health visitors have some of the knowledge about sections of the profile, particularly in relation to health status, experiences and needs, it is not until that information is pooled that patterns and trends can be identified. It is only when a pattern is identified, such as an increase in the number of women experiencing postnatal depression, that action can be taken.

Good starting points for gathering information about statistics and services include:

1 Local libraries.
2 Health education departments.
3 Voluntary services councils.

4 Health authority statistic units.
5 Community medicine departments.
6 Local authority planning departments.
7 Local authority information units.
8 Community health councils.

Of equal importance is speaking to local people and professionals about their perceptions of an area and the health of its residents. Obvious starting points include:

1 People in health visitor case loads.
2 Clinic or surgery users.
3 Ancillary staff in the clinic or surgery.
4 Other health service staff.
5 Social workers.
6 Community workers.
7 Religious leaders.
8 Child care/play workers.

In exploring an area and talking to people health visitors are beginning to establish a network of contacts. Making links with people in an area is vital to any health visiting practice and particularly to working with groups. Getting to know people involves more than a one-off meeting when you are looking for information. It takes time and evolves out of repeated meetings. It is important to work at making a network of contacts and building good relationships. There is a variety of ways in which this can happen and the following are some examples:

1 Attending community forums arranged by councils for voluntary services or other such bodies These are often lunch-time meetings organised around a theme with the intention of creating a dialogue between different organisations in a community. They are usually attended by people from statutory and voluntary organisations.
2 Attending forums of professionals and other interested parties which focus on a particular issue, such as a housing estate or under-5 provision. The purpose of these sessions is to introduce lay and professional people

to each other, to develop clearer understandings of each other's role and perceptions and to provide a talking point for developing new ideas. If there are no forums like this in the area perhaps there is scope for developing one.

3 Inviting staff from other organisations and disciplines to regular informal lunches at the clinic or health centre to meet the health visitors and talk about common interests and roles.

4 Setting up a series of formal meetings between health visitors based in one clinic and another local organisation, such as a social work team or child guidance centre, to explain about each other's roles, perceptions and working methods.

5 Regularly dropping in to community organisations in the geographical area or, if health visitors are GP-attached, designating a cluster to each. This means going to meet people on a regular basis, not just when there is a problem to be discussed or when a favour is wanted. It also means expanding horizons beyond those organisations which are solely concerned with under-5 provision.

It is only by developing these relationships that health visitors can begin to work with people in response to their needs and tap into the resources and expertise of other organisations and disciplines. In meeting people, collecting information and working with clients, health visitors will begin to identify health needs, such as a need for a weekend well baby clinic, or under-5 play facilities, a support group for recently bereaved people or relief for carers of elderly relatives. Health visitors who have established networks of contacts will have a starting point from which to join with other people in responding to health needs.

JOINING IN

By making networks of contacts health visitors can begin to develop roles in different types of group activity. The case studies in this book show the different ways in which health visitors can join together to respond to health needs. Broadly speaking, they have described how health visitors can use group work in health education (in its widest sense), how they can work in groups to influence policy and service and how they can use groups to enhance their own professional practice. The following are some examples of various roles in which health visitors can be engaged:

1 They can become resources of information for already established groups by frequently dropping in and spending time with the group in an informal way.
2 They can have a more defined relationship with an established group whereby they have a regular commitment to attend and lead discussions on health.
3 They can become known to an established group so that they can be called on to lead a discussion on health as and when required.
4 They can support an established group by directing potential new members to it.
5 They can help to establish new groups and forums.
6 They can support campaigns and pressure groups.
7 They can work with others to plan and develop new services.

In many situations the act of joining in and working with others will be much more positive than attempting to start something new. Many established forums and groups welcome the involvement of health visitors. The skills necessary for each activity listed above are very different and can often only be learnt by experience. They can also be learnt from the example of others and by consulting more experienced people during the process. To become successfully involved in groups many health visitors will have to rethink their own position. They will have to consider moving away from more traditional ideas, for example, that the health professional has all the knowledge which must not be questioned, and that the health visitor's role in promoting health means lecturing people who passively accept her expertise.

STARTING A GROUP

In contemplating starting a group the first thing to do is to ask why? It may help to clarify the question by writing down the reasons. The following questions may help:

1 Is there a need that has been identified?
2 How has the need been identified?
3 Is the formation of a group the only solution?
4 What other ways are there of responding to the need?
5 Have people expressed the desire for some sort of group?
6 Is there already a group responding to that need?

If, after answering these questions, it becomes clear that the sole reason is that one person — i.e. the health visitor — feels it would be a good idea but there is no evidence to suggest that anyone else does, then she needs to go back to her network of contacts, both lay and professional. She must start discussing the idea with other people to establish that this is what people want and that they are prepared to be involved.

Once she has clarified her thoughts about why this group would be a good response she needs to examine more closely what the purpose of the group would be. This is the initial stage in defining aims and objectives. The aims are likely to be much wider than the objectives. The following questions may help to identify the initial aims. In answering, it may become clear that discussions with potential group members will be necessary to identify aims and objectives: what do they want out of the group?

1 Are people looking for information?
2 Do they want to find strategies for coping?
3 Do they need to meet other people in a similar situation?
4 Do they want to learn new skills or practise old ones?
5 Are people looking for new facilities or services?
6 Do they want a social encounter?
7 Do they want opportunities to exercise?
8 Are they looking for a therapeutic encounter?
9 Do people want several of these things or one in isolation?

Example

A health visitor who visits a large number of elderly people notices that there are several households in which she spends most of her visit advising and listening to a relative who is caring for a severely disabled person. She notices that these carers have some common needs — the main one being to talk to another adult about how they feel. One of these carers says how much she would like to talk to other people in her situation. The health visitor discusses this with the district nurse based in her clinic. The district nurse is also aware of a number of carers who need support and information about services, allowances etc. They both agree that a group which gives carers the opportunity to come together to talk about their problems and develop solutions for coping would be a positive response to the need. Neither of them knows of one in existence and enquiries to the Council of Voluntary Services, a local pensioners' organisation and the social work team concerned with elderly people do not reveal one. However one of the social workers has encountered people with similar needs and is interested in helping establish such a group. The three professionals meet together and decide to hold an initial meeting of carers living in the immediate area. They decide it should be a mid-afternoon meeting lasting 1 hour and they will personally invite people. The purpose of this meeting will be to explore the need for such a group and then plan with the carers the format, membership and activities of the group. They go away to invite individuals to the meeting. They arrange to meet again to discuss responses to the invitation and plan the detailed arrangements for the meeting.

Staffing

Having identified the need to establish a group, the health visitor then needs to think about her role and commitment. To some extent the purpose of the group will determine her role. For example, a self-help group may only need her to be a facilitator in initially bringing people together or negotiating meeting space in the clinic. It may be that the group is coming together for a short health course and she may be leading the discussions at each meeting. There are two important aspects she needs to consider. The first is how much time and energy she is prepared to devote to this enterprise. In thinking this through she needs to discuss her commitment with close colleagues and her manager. She will need their support not just in practical details but in organising her work. If the group is to meet in the evening then she will need to be assured that she can claim time-in-lieu during the daytime. Colleagues may need to be prepared to cover during holidays or illness as well as being informed about the new group. Group work is demanding of time and energy and deserves to be treated with equal importance as individual work. From the start, time needs to be clearly set aside for preparation and being with the group and nothing should be allowed to diminish that.

The second aspect to be considered is that it is usually more successful to work with other people in establishing or facilitating a group. These people could be professionals and/or lay people. By working as a team, albeit a small one, the feelings of being part of a group and not an isolated individual begin to develop. Practical reasons for working with others include the sharing of skills, ideas and tasks as well as being able to evaluate situations from different perspectives. It may be that different roles are needed in establishing the group, for example, someone who encourages other people to attend, someone who leads particular activities, someone who is skilled at facilitating discussions about intimate feelings. It may also be important that all or some of the initial or key people involved have particular attributes because of the nature of the group. These attributes may include gender, race, class, personal experience or ability to speak another language.

Example

Two detached youth workers realise from their conversations with young men and women how little factual information many of these young people have about the way their bodies work, how diseases are transmitted — especially sexually transmitted diseases — and how confused some of them are about relationships, sexuality and sex. They talk with the young people and determine that some of them would like to meet to talk about health issues. However the young women do not want to talk when young men are present and many of the young men are flippant about the whole idea. The youth workers then approach the local health visitor and suggest that they jointly lead a series of discussions in a youth club. They feel they have complementary skills and knowledge in leading the discussions. As a result of their relationships with the young people they feel that it would be better if there were separate parallel sessions for each sex led by a youth worker and health visitor of the same sex. However there are no male health visitors in that health district so the health visitor contacts a male district nurse and a male health adviser from the genitourinary clinic to ask whether either of them would become involved.

The building up of trust and the negotiating of roles between those who are establishing a group is essential. To work effectively together they need to agree a frame of reference concerning their purpose and methods. For example, if a health visitor believes that the purpose of setting up a post-natal group is to teach women how to care for a newborn baby, but the local mother with whom she is working believes that the group is about giving women the opportunity to talk about their feelings and make friends, then there will be obvious conflicts and disappointments unless they openly talk through these differences before they embark on the venture.

Membership

It will be fairly obvious who the potential members will be once the aims of the group have been clarified — whether it is to increase children's knowledge about their health (a children's health club after school), or break down the isolation of elderly people from the Caribbean (a Caribbean pensioners' forum) or to provide opportunities for support for bereaved parents (a bereaved parents' group). What does need consideration is the group size and whether the membership is to be open or closed. Open groups are those which welcome new members at any time; closed groups restrict their membership. Again it is the purpose of the group which will decide these factors. If the group is intended to provide security, intimacy and the development of very close relationships then an open membership would prove disruptive. Welcoming new members and losing established members at different points in the group's life can create difficulties in a more 'therapeutic' group. Open groups must consider how new members are welcomed. It takes a great deal of personal confidence to join an established group unless welcoming strategies are well thought out.

The size of a group will depend on its purpose. If the activity of the group is concerned with general and social matters then size is not really important, as large groups will easily break down into smaller groups. If the activity of the group is concerned with giving people the opportunity to speak and share experiences then the larger the group, the less time individuals will have to speak. Large groups can be intimidating, making it difficult for individuals with less confidence to speak. Where personal contact is important more than 15 people become problematic.

Activities

As has already been stated, the initial aims of the group and the introductory meetings will help point to the types of activities in which group members want to participate. Group work in health means that members are active in planning and participating. There is an emphasis on sharing and co-operation between members and health visitor. The aims are much more about raising awareness, fostering support and developing confidence rather than just increasing knowledge. The following are some of the possible activities groups may undertake:

1 Inviting specialist speakers.
2 Discussing a topic introduced by a health visitor.
3 Watching and discussing videos.
4 Sharing experiences.
5 Role-playing.
6 Making their own video or tape slide on a topic.
7 Producing their own leaflets, pamphlets or directories.
8 Learning practical skills.
9 Learning relaxation or massage skills.
10 Exercising.
11 Organising or participating in a health festival.

Groups may be formed to influence policies and services. Their activities are likely to include some of the following:

1 Surveying local people's opinions.
2 Collecting information.
3 Writing reports.
4 Presenting reports to influential people.
5 Organising petitions.
6 Drawing up plans or schemes.
7 Fund-raising.
8 Lobbying influential people, such as local councillors or health authority members.
9 Holding public meetings.

Whatever the activities are to be, the health visitor needs to think through her role, and what contribution she will make and prepare herself well in advance.

Attracting Members

A number of methods for attracting members need to be considered. In general, small local groups usually gain their members by word of mouth and personal invitation rather than by public posters and leaflets. People often need the security of knowing someone who will be present before they will come to a meeting. They also may need the reassurance of knowing what sort of things will happen and that there will be something positive for them in attending a group. For health visitors this may mean talking to people in their case load and explaining about the group. It also means using their network of contacts to tell people about the group. For this to work effectively the health visitor will have to spend time talking to key people and colleagues, explaining in detail about the group and getting them to promote it with possibly interested people. A referral system may be a very beneficial strategy when the membership has particular characteristics or problems in common.

Example

A health visitor and a local woman (from her case load) who had experienced a sudden infant death 4 years previously felt there was a need to establish a support group for similarly bereaved parents. They felt it should be an open group because there is no way of predicting when the bereavement might happen or when parents decide they want to share their feelings with others in a similar situation. They decided that it would be helpful in welcoming new members to the group to make sure that during their first attendance they had an opportunity to speak about themselves — whether it was a few sentences or much more would be up to them. They felt that the group should be relatively small so that everyone would have time to speak if they wished. Although posters and leaflets might be important in attracting members they felt that personal invitations and referrals would be much more effective. The health visitor then spent time in unit meetings explaining about the group to other health visitor and school nurse colleagues. She also spoke to the permanent hospital staff in the paediatric unit and accident and emergency department. The mother spoke about the group to her neighbours and friends. She also spoke about it to staff and parents at the school and playgroup where her children attended. The referral system they set up meant that the sister on the paediatric ward, with the permission of a recently bereaved couple, contacted the health visitor. The health visitor (although it could equally have been the mother) then arranged to meet the parents and talk about the group, inviting them to the next meeting.

Publicity

A useful source of expertise and materials for producing publicity materials will be the local Heath Education Department. There may also be other local resources, such as community printshops, and the council for voluntary services may help. In producing publicity materials two things need to be considered: what is on the publicity and what is going to happen to it? In designing publicity the following checklist will help get the essentials right:

1 Is it bright and eye-catching?
2 Is the lettering bold?
3 Does it need to be in more than one language?
4 Does it have the date, time and place?
5 Does it need a map?
6 Does it explain what will happen in the meetings?
7 Does it state what sort of people it is intended for?
8 Does it state whether membership is free or not?
9 Does it state whether there is a crêche available?

When displaying publicity it is worth considering who it is intended to attract and then placing the posters and leaflets in the most appropriate places. There is no point putting posters all over a town if the group is intended to be local to a particular neighbourhood. Leafleting outside a post office on pension day may be more effective than fly-posting an estate if the group is for elderly people.

Finally, because of the nature of the group, the potential members may come from a very wide area. It may therefore be worth thinking about approaching the local press and radio to help publicise the group. They may have community noticeboard sections or may consider doing a feature from a press release. Further information on this aspect can be found in the section on useful reading. It is also worth noting that the Health Visitors' Association runs courses on how to use the media.

PRACTICAL DETAILS IN PLANNING

Place

A wide variety of venues may be suitable for holding group meetings. It is only by making contacts that it is possible to determine what is available in a locality. Possible venues include:

1 Child health clinic.
2 Member's front room.
3 Local church hall.
4 Community centre.
5 Library.
6 Village hall.
7 Sports centre.
8 Adult education centre.

A number of questions need to be examined in relation to choosing a venue for a group; once again it comes back to the purpose of the group and who will be attending. The following list of questions will help establish a suitable venue:

1 It is easy for prospective members to get to?
2 Will it cost to hire the room and if so, where is the money coming from?
3 Is there good access to the building and room for buggies, wheelchairs etc?
4 Are there toilet facilities and are these suitable for people with mobility problems?
5 Is there access to refreshment facilities?

6 Does the room have the right atmosphere? Is it small and intimate or huge and barn-like?
7 Does the room have good acoustics, light, heating and ventilation?
8 Does it have the facilities the group needs, such as carpets for relaxation exercises or a separate room for children?
9 Is there insurance cover for any possible accidents?

For many groups there are few choices of venue but it is worth considering the needs of the group and exploring all local possibilities.

Time

The time of day and the day of week will need careful consideration in relation to who the prospective members are. Evenings may be unsuitable for elderly people, while day times will be unsuitable for people who are in employment. Weekends may be more possible for people with heavy work and family commitments. When launching a group the time of year needs to be considered. Holiday periods and winter months when there is bad weather and dark evenings tend to discourage people from becoming involved in something new. The length of time of each session needs to be considered in relation to what the possible activities are. Exercises, discussions, informal chat and tea breaks will all involve different lengths of time. The period of time for which the group will run will need consideration. If it is to be more like a health course then it may initially be quite short, say over 5 or 6 weeks, with the intention of continuing if there is the impetus. A support group will have a much longer projected life span.

Transport

When the venue is chosen factors such as public transport and locality are looked at. However it may be that transport or escorts will have to be arranged for a number of reasons.

The locality may be a rural area where public transport is negligible and communities spread out. It may be that members are afraid to come out alone during the day or in the evenings. There may also be members who have mobility problems. Possible solutions include:

1 Members calling for or picking each other up.
2 Volunteer car drivers from a local volunteer bureau.
3 Using a minibus to collect and return members. These may be available on loan from a community centre, youth group, social services or a community transport service.

Back-up Facilities

In order to attend or to become fully involved in the group meeting it may be that members will need certain support facilities, such as a crêche or home sitters for elderly relatives. A crêche needs a separate space (with extra consideration of safety), play materials and people to be with the children. Talking with people in relevant organisations, such as volunteer bureaux, child care provision and pensioners' organisations, may reveal possible sources of staffing and equipment locally. It is possible that there is a mobile crêche or a network of volunteer home sitters available in the area. It may be that local volunteers or staff have to be sought and funding gained or contributions asked for to cover costs and expenses.

Finance

Finance will need some consideration, even if it is only concerned with where the money will come from to buy the teabags for the first meeting. Some groups will have expenditure, such as for hiring a room or staffing a crêche. Sometimes health visitors have access to small amounts of money through petty cash available to the community nurses in clinics but greater expenditure will need a more substantial source. Senior nurses may know of money available within the health district for certain types of activities. Other organisations or charities in the area may have funds available that can be utilised. Again it comes down to making use of the network of contacts and other people's expertise in locating an appropriate source of funds. If there is to be payment by the members for refreshments or crèche facilities or just donations towards costs then someone has to be responsible for ensuring the money is collected and dealt with.

Tasks

One important area that needs to be decided well in advance of the meeting is who will be responsible for what tasks, and checking that these members have been well prepared. The planners or organisers of the group must ensure that they have discussed their individual inputs and responsibilities. The following list includes some of the main tasks that need to be allocated in advance:

1 Arranging chairs and the room.
2 Welcoming people.
3 Arrangements for refreshments and paying.
4 Clearing up.
5 Organising and checking equipment like videos, kettles etc.
6 Starting and ending the meeting.
7 Asking people for their names and addresses.

    This is not an exhaustive list but does include some of the things that tend to be forgotten.

Materials and Resources

Materials on aspects of health, such as videos, leaflets and tapes or slides, are widely used within groups. However, a number of points need to be considered about their use.

Firstly, it is important to recognise that people are the biggest resource of knowledge and ideas available. People are not empty vessels, without information or perceptions, waiting to be filled with complete new ideas. Utilising each other's perceptions and experiences is often more valuable than watching a video. That is not to say that health education materials do not have an important place, but that place is within the context of people talking and sharing.

For health visitors the most obvious source of these materials will be the district health education or health promotion unit. Another source might be the local library, which will often lend a selection of books to a particular group. In using any materials on health it is important that they should be scrutinised carefully beforehand to ensure they contain accurate information; that they are relevant to the people who will be using them; that they do not portray negative stereotyping of age, race, gender, class or ability and that they use understandable language. It is important to note that there is no perfect resource as each group of people will have a slightly different focus and need. Often there are no suitable materials available to help stimulate discussions but health education officers may know of other materials that can be ordered or borrowed from elsewhere. The solution may be to produce new handouts or leaflets, and again health education units usually have the staff and facilities to help health visitors and group members do this. Getting to know the staff and facilities of the health education department will prove very valuable to any health visitors working with groups.

Some people seem to feel that showing a video or film is the best way of transmitting information about health topics but the reality is that watching videos is a passive activity and much more thought needs to be given to how that film will stimulate interaction. The following questions may help the health visitor use audiovisual materials more effectively. The last two questions are the most important and apply to all materials used:

1   Does the venue have equipment? If not, where will it come from and how will it be returned?

2   If slides or films are to be used, will there be adequate darkness or a daylight screen?
3   Does someone know how to check and use the equipment?
4   What will happen if there is a problem?
5   Have the resources been reviewed and timed?
6   How will the audiovisual material stimulate discussion?
7   How will it be introduced and how will discussion start afterwards?

LIFE SPAN OF A GROUP

This section is concerned with the practical aspects of the life of a group. It does not attempt to deal with the interpersonal relationships, communication skills and changing experiences in the group. These aspects of group dynamics are covered in many other books, some of which are listed in the section on useful reading. Some health visitors may find it helpful to attend a short course on this aspect. These tend to be run by health education departments, local councils for voluntary organisations and adult education institutes. If there are none available it may be worthwhile approaching the health education department or the post-basic education service in your health district to ask for such a course.

It is a common experience of most groups that they begin with a very small number of interested people. Groups often experience an upsurge in numbers followed by a dwindling away and settle to a relatively small number. Building up the membership can be quite a slow process which needs a lot of work. Small numbers should not be viewed as failure as some groups, such as those whose primary aims are support or self-help, may work more effectively this way. However it may be a situation that needs more thought and investigation. The following questions may help to decide how to deal with it:

1   Do people come once and not return?
2   Is it possible to contact those people and ask why they have stopped coming?

3 Would the group feel comfortable with more members?
4 Does the group work better together with small numbers?
5 Have the activities or aims of the group changed from the original publicity?

The decision to follow up people who have stopped attending can be quite hard as it often feels quite intrusive, but it may be that these people have observations which will help the group welcome and retain members in the future. It may be that they found it difficult to join in with established members or they arrived expecting one sort of activity, only to find that it no longer occurred.

The work of attracting members needs to continue after the initial meetings. A re-examination of publicity materials, referral systems and personal invitations to the group may be useful in helping to improve ways of interesting new members. Perhaps the posters should be redesigned or put up in different places, perhaps the members should try to introduce a neighbour or friend to the group, or perhaps relevant key referral people should be contacted again.

As a group grows and develops other situations may arise. Two such problems are that the group has too many members and that the members have different interests. The solution may be to change the organisation of the meetings so that subgroups can meet in different rooms for part of the session. Meeting more frequently can also help alleviate these situations. Of course, setting up sister groups may be a more practical way forward. These may be in different neighbourhoods or meet at a different time. It may be that these sister groups aim to provide for different interests or activities.

Another possible situation is that the group's aims may alter with time. This may happen unconsciously or after a meeting when a conscious decision to change is taken. One example of this is when original members of a post-natal support group, after some months of meeting (and the post-natal period receding), decided they would like to learn more about their children's development. They decided to follow the Open University Course on pre-school children.

Change is often beneficial. However this change has to be made clear to potential new members, who can be confused and disappointed to find their chosen group has evolved into something totally different.

It is important to stop and review the activities of the group as a whole at regular intervals. One result may be the ending of the group. Groups come and go and many have a natural life span that should not be extended. The ending of a group can be a very positive step. If the group achieves its aims then there is no purpose in continuing to meet. Some groups are established for a set number of meetings, particularly those that are seen more as a health course. On the more negative side, there are groups which fail to attract new members and the original members just fade away, or where personality conflicts and strongly held views lead people to leave. Whatever the reasons, the ending of a group should be dealt with positively. There should always be a final meeting in which the group appraises its achievements, looking at strengths and weaknesses. The benefits of this are that group members are able to say goodbye properly and make positive decisions. Some may wish to continue seeing each other; others can be directed to other activities or groups. For the health visitor it will also be a means of saying goodbye and of using the appraisal to enhance her future professional activities.

Example

A health visitor, a community worker and two local women planned to establish a women's health group on a housing estate. The first two meetings were very poorly attended. Together with the two or three women who did attend they discussed why this might be so. They decided to spend some time talking about the group to women they knew and bring other women along with them. At the next session there were several new members. Over the next 2 months a core membership of 14 women was established and several more women attended once or twice. After 5 months of weekly meetings the membership began to fade away. The original planners discussed this with the group members who were still participating and agreed to contact those who were no longer attending to find out why. From their investigations it became clear that many of the women felt that they had got what they wanted from that group — whether it was information, confidence, friendship or support. At the next meeting with the remaining few they all discussed this. They all felt that the group should end in that format but that there might be a possibility of establishing something different in the near future, like a massage course, as several women had expressed interest in massage. They felt there should be a proper ending to the group and decided to have a social meeting, like a party, the following week and personally invited all those that used to attend. In this final meeting they planned to get everyone to talk about the good and bad things that had happened in the group. They also planned to sound out the idea of a massage course.

EVALUATION

Good evaluation assesses what has been achieved against what was intended and explains why this happened in order to derive some lessons for future work. It is about measuring change and making changes to approach more nearly the core purpose of the work (Graessle and Kingsley, 1986).

The very idea of evaluation is daunting to many health visitors, yet in reality it is an everyday activity. Most health visitors are constantly appraising their work — what worked, what did not work, why it worked and how it could be done better in the future. This section applies those questions to working with groups. It may be important to have a written report of the evaluation. This could be used in clarifying the achievements for managers. It may also be useful to circulate it to other health visitors as part of a learning process for them. Documentation of the process and outcome is a means of accountability as well as publicity for the work of health visitors.

The basis of the evaluation should come from the aims and objectives of the work. Questions are derived from these aims and objectives to form the framework of the evaluation. For example, a health visitor established a menopause support group which had the aims of:

1 Enabling women to understand more about the physical, emotional and social effects of the climacteric.
2 Enabling women to learn about medical treatments and complementary therapies available.
3 Enabling women to share experience and thereby gain support.

The basic questions of her evaluation are:

1 Did they have a greater understanding of the physical, emotional and social effects of the climacteric?
2 Did they have a greater knowledge about medical treatments and complementary therapies?
3 Did they share experiences?
4 Did they gain support from each other?
5 If these things happened, how did they happen?

Once the questions became clear then the method of finding out the answers will also become clearer. The variety of methods includes questionnaires, surveys, interviews, being an impartial observer of events, recording group sessions on tape or in a diary. Different methods suit different situations. Time constraints will also dictate method. Health visitors can often get help in developing a system of evaluation from health visitor colleagues who have more experience of social science research, from nursing research departments and community nurse researchers. Whichever method is used, it is important to create time to record events and information as they happen. Memory is an unreliable storage system for reports written months after the events.

The following list (adapted from Graessle and Kingsley, 1986) may help health visitors establish their own evaluation programme:

1 Identify the questions.
2 Break them down into their smallest component parts.

3 Develop a recording system.
4 Set a time limit.
5 Review answers periodically.
6 Modify work as appropriate.
7 Analyse results for the entire period.
8 Present results in the most appropriate format.

Support

Linked closely with the evaluation process is the health visitor's need for supervisory support. The purpose of supervisory support is to provide a time when the health visitor -(and others involved in leading or establishing the group) can share with someone who is not directly involved with the events, process and development of that group. It is an opportunity to evaluate different aspects of the health visitor's role and the achievements of the group. It is also an opportunity to plan modifications or new initiatives. The 'outsider' is able to provide a detached point of view when looking at the group overall. This person is also able to offer regular support and guidance to the health visitor. How often they meet together depends on the confidence and experience of the health visitor. The frequency may change according to her needs but what is important is that the meetings are regular so that evaluation, support and guidance can take place. The impartial supervisor must be someone who has experience of group work. This could be another health visitor, senior nurse, community worker or health education officer. A health visitor will get informal support from her colleagues and managerial support from her senior nurse but she will also need the opportunity to evaluate situations and develop strategies for dealing with problems with someone who is experienced in group work.

CONCLUSIONS

This chapter has given basic practical suggestions for health visitors interested in developing their role with community groups. It has focused to a large extent on the health visitor's role with groups in health but has also touched on using groups to develop health visiting practice and to influence services. Becoming involved with groups is both challenging and stimulating for health visitors. The personal and professional rewards from such activities are enormous. The outcomes of this type of work can have far-reaching effects for the health of individuals and communities. To be true promoters of health for all ages and all parts of the community, health visitors must diversify their activities and start working in a different way.

References

Albany Health Project (1983). *The First Five Years*. Albany Health Project, London.

Allen, W., King, V., Abbott, G. (1969). *Survey of Work Undertaken by Domiciliary Nurses*. Unpublished. Hereford County Council.

Baldock, P. (1980). The origins of community work. In: Henderson, P. *et al.* (eds.) *The Boundaries of Change in Community Work*. National Institute Social Services Library No. 37.

Balter, D., Daniels, F., Finch, J., Perkins, E. (1986). *Training Health Visitors to Work with Community Groups*. University of Nottingham Department of Adult Education/Nottingham and Bassetlaw Health Education Unit, Nottingham.

Beattie, A. (1985). Evaluation in practice. In: Somerville, G. (ed.) *Addressing the Confusions*. King's Fund Centre, London.

Biggs, S. (1986). *Personal Communication*. Bloomsbury Health Authority, London.

Billingham, K. (1986). *Personal Communication*. Nottingham Health Authority, Nottingham.

Blaxter, M., Patterson, E. (1982). *Mothers and Daughters: A Three-generational Study of Health Attitudes and Behaviour*. Heinemann, London.

Brent Community Health Council (1981). *Black People and the Health Service*. Brent CHC, London.

Bristol Child Development Project (1984). *Child Development Programme*. Early Childhood Development Unit, University of Bristol.

Burford Nursing Development Unit (1985). Newsletter. *Nursing Times*; **81**: 42.

Butler, J., Vaile, M. (1984). *Health and the Health Services: An Introduction to Health Care in Britain*. Routledge & Kegan Paul, London.

Central Statistical Office (1984). *Social Trends 14*, HMSO, London.

Central Statistical Office (1985). *Social Trends 15*, HMSO, London.
City of Newcastle (1974). *Social Characteristics of Newcastle upon Tyne*. City of Newcastle, Newcastle.
Clark, J. (1983). Evaluating health visiting practice. *Health Visitor*; **56**: 205–8.
Clarkson, G. (1982). The role of community projects foundation. In: *Community Development: Towards a National Perspective*. Community Projects Foundation, London.
Colver, A. (1984). Community campaign against asthma. *Archives of Disease in Childhood*; **59**: 449–52.
Community Development Projects (1977). *Gilding the Ghetto*. Community Projects Foundation, London.
Community Health Initiatives Resource Unit/London Community Health Resource (CHIRU/LCHR) (1987a). *Guide to Community Health Projects*. CHIRU/LCHR, London.
CHIRU/LCHR (1987b). *Report of the First National Community Health Action Conference*. CHIRU/LCHR, London.
Community Projects Foundation (1982). *Community Development: Towards a National Perspective*. Community Projects Foundation, London.
Council for the Education and Training of Health Visitors (CETHV) (1977). *An Investigation into the Principles of Health Visiting*. CETHV, London.
Cox, M. (1983). A health and social club for the middle-aged and elderly. *Health Visitor*; **56**: 301.
Cox, C., Mead, A. (eds.) (1975). *A Sociology of Medical Practice*. Collier Macmillan, London.
Crawford, R. (1979). You are dangerous to your health: the ideology of victim blaming. *International Journal of Health Services*; **9**: 663.
Davidson, D. (1987). Burnt out cases? *Health Visitor*; **60**: 51.
Department of Environment (1983). *Urban Deprivation*. Information note no. 2. Inner Cities Directorate, Department of Environment, London.
DHSS (1974). *Fit for the Future*. Report of the committee on the child health services. HMSO, London.
DHSS (1976a). *Priorities for the Health and Personal Social Services in England*. HMSO, London.
DHSS (1976b). *Prevention and Health: Everybody's Business*. HMSO, London.
DHSS (1977). *The Way Forward*. HMSO, London.
DHSS (1978). *A Happier Old Age*. HMSO, London.
DHSS (1980). *Inequalities in Health*: Report of a Research Working Group. HMSO, London.

DHSS (1981). *Care in Action*. HMSO, London.
DHSS (1983). *Steering Group on Health Services Information:* a report from a working group on community health services. HMSO, London.
DHSS (1986). *Neighbourhood Nursing — a Focus for Care*. HMSO, London.
Dingwall, R. (1976). Collectivism, regionalism and feminism. *Journal of Social Policy*; **6**: 291–315.
Dobby, J., Barnes, A. (1986). Measuring the need for, and the value of, routine health visiting 1 and 2. *Health Visitor*; **60**: 81–2; 114–5.
Downham, M., White, M., Moss, T. (1980). A study of childhood morbidity and mortality in relation to the provision of child health services in Newcastle upon Tyne. *Health Trends*; **12**: 4.
Doyal, L. (1979). *The Political Economy of Health*. Pluto Press, London.
Draper, P., Ambler, M., Lewis, J., Anderson, J. (1969). Health visiting after Seebohm. *Nursing Times*; **65**: 40–1; 82–3; 114–15.
Drennan, V. (1985). *Working in a Different Way*. Paddington and North Kensington Community Nursing Unit, London.
Drennan, V. (1986a). *Effective Health Education in the Inner City*. Paddington and North Kensington Health Education Unit, London.
Drennan, V. (1986b). Developments in health visiting. *Health Visitor*; **59**: 108–10.
Drennan, V. (1987). Working in a different way. *Senior Nurse*; **6**: 11–13.
Drennan, V., McGeeney, S. (1985). Menopausal support. *Nursing Mirror*; **160**: 27–8.
Drennan, V., Stearn, J. (1986). Health visitors and homeless families. *Health Visitor*; **59**: 340–2.
Drummond, G. (1984). Laughter is the best medicine: a support group for caring relatives. *Health Visitor*; **57**: 201–2.
Farnese. M. (1979). Belonging in suburbia. *Nursing Mirror*; **149**: 38.
Fitton, J. (1981). How am I doing as a health teacher? *Nursing Times*; **77**: 85–6.
Forester, S. (1981). *Unpublished Paper*. Great Chapel St. Medical Centre, London.
Fothergill, S., Vincent, J. (1985). *The State of the Nation*. Heinemann, London.
Furlong, E. N. (1975). A mothers' group in Alperton. *Nursing Mirror*; **140**: 70.
Gillmore, F. (1983). Shape up for health education. *Nursing Mirror*; **156**: 34–5.
Graessle, L., Kingsley, S. (1986). *Measuring Change, Making*

Changes. London Community Health Resource, London.

Graham, H. (1985). *Women, Health and the Family.* Wheatsheaf Books, Sussex.

Graham, H., McKee, L. (1979). *The First Months of Motherhood.* Health Education Council, London.

Gregory, S. (1982). Discussion groups for mothers. *Nursing Times;* **78**: 2085–6.

Grimley Evans, J. (1981). Demographic implications for planning services in the United Kingdom. In: Kinnaird, J., Brotherston, J., Williamson, J. (eds.) *The Provision of Care for the Elderly.* Churchill Livingstone, Edinburgh.

Halner, J., Rose, H. (1980). Making sense of theory. In: Henderson, P. *et al.* (eds.) *The Boundaries of Change in Community Work.* National Institute Social Services Library no. 37.

Harrison, J. (1986). *The Workloads of Health Visitors in Sheffield.* Sheffield Community Nursing Service, Sheffield.

Harwood, K. (1966). Is it time for a new title? *Nursing Mirror;* **121**: 538.

Health Visitors' Association (1985) *Health Visiting and School Nursing: The Future.* HVA, London.

Henderson, P. *et al.* (eds.) (1980) *The Boundaries of Change in Community Work.* National Institute Social Services Library no. 37. Allen & Unwin, London.

Hennessey, D., Holgate, B., Marr, J. (1978). With a little help from my friends. *Community Outlook;* **74**: 103–6.

Hiskins, G., (1983). Post-natal support groups. In: Clark, J., Henderson, J. (eds.) *Community Health.* Churchill Livingstone, Edinburgh.

Hobbs, P. (1973). *Aptitude or Environment?* Royal College of Nursing, London.

Hubley, J. (1980). Community development and health education. *Journal of the Institute of Health Education;* **18**: 113–20.

Hunt, M. (1972). The dilemma of identity in health visiting. *Nursing Times;* occasional papers nos. 5 and 6.

Illich, I. (1975). *Limits to Medicine.* Marion Boyars, London.

Jefferies, M. (1965). The uncertain health visitor. *New Society;* Oct. 26: 16–18.

Kennedy, I. (1981). *The Unmasking of Medicine.* Allen & Unwin, London.

Kenner, C. (1986). *Whose Needs Count?* Bedford Square Press/ NCVO, London.

Kewley, J. (1983). The health visitor as catalyst. *Health Visitor;* **56**: 443.

Klein, R. (1984) 1000 projects blossom. *Health and Social Services*

Journal; April 12: 442.

Klein, R., Lewis, J. (1976). *The Politics of Consumer Representation*. Centre for Studies in Social Policy, London.

London Council for Social Service (1979). *Evaluation of Community Work*. London Council of Social Service, London.

Luker, K. (1982a). Screening of the well-elderly in general practice. *Midwife, Health Visitor and Community Nurse*; **18**: 222–9.

Luker, K. (1982b). *Evaluating Health Visiting Practice*. RCN, London.

Luker, K. (1985). Evaluating health visiting practice. In: Luker, K., Orr, J. (eds.) *Health Visiting*. Blackwell Scientific Publications, Oxford.

Luker, K., Orr, J. (1985) *Health Visiting*. Blackwell Scientific Publications, Oxford.

McCleary, G. F. (1935). *The Maternity and Child Health Movement*. King, London.

McIntosh, J. (1985). *A Consumer Perspective on the Health Visiting Service*. Department of Child Health and Obstetrics, University of Glasgow, Glasgow.

McKeown, T. (1976). *The Role of Medicine*. Blackwell, London.

Mayo, M. (1975). The history and early development of community development projects. In: Less, R., Smith, G. (eds.) *Action Research in Community Development*. Routledge & Kegan Paul, London.

Mitchell, J. (1984). *What is to be Done About Illness and Health?* Penguin, Middlesex.

Morris, R. (1985). *The Need for Community Development in Health* (conference paper). CHIRU/LCHR, London.

Moulds, V., Hennessey, D., Crack, P., Murray, M. (1983). An adult health group. *Health Visitor*; **56**: 297–8.

Newell, G. (1984). Working in a well woman clinic. *Health Visitor*; **57**: 207–8.

Nurses' Reference Library (1984). *Definitions*. Nursing 84 Books, Springhouse, Pennsylvania.

Orr, J. (1980). *Health Visiting in Focus*. RCN, London.

Orr, J. (1983). Health visiting in the UK. In: Hockney, L. (ed.) *Primary Care Nursing*. Churchill Livingstone, Edinburgh.

Orr, J. (1985). The community dimension. In: Luker, K., Orr, J. (eds.) *Health Visiting*. Blackwell Scientific Publications, Oxford.

Osman, T. (1985). *The Facts of Everyday Life*. Faber & Faber, London.

Paddington and North Kensington Health Authority (1985). *Health Profile*. Department of Community Medicine, Paddington and North Kensington Health Authority, London.

Pearson, P. (1983). Health visiting in inner city districts. *Community Nurse, Health Visitor and Midwife*; **20**: 196–8.

Pearson, P. (1984). Images of a health visitor. *Nursing Mirror*; **159**: 21–3.

Pearson, P. (1985a). Health reviews in nursery school. *Health Visitor*; **58**: 291–2.

Pearson, P. (1985b). Parent held records — what parents think. *Health Visitor*; **58**: 15–16.

Pensioners' Link, Brent (1984). *Is it Just my Age?* Pensioners' Link, Brent.

Perkins, E. (1978). *Group Health Education by Health Visitors.* Occasional paper no. 7. Leverhulme Health Education Project, University of Nottingham, Nottingham.

Phillips, S. (1986). A centre for change? *Community Outlook*; February; 15–17.

Pollitt, C. (1985). *Evaluation of the Community Health Projects in Walker, North Kenton and Riverside.* Riverside Child Health Project, Newcastle on Tyne.

Radical Health Visitors' Group. *All Publications.* Reference copies held in the Health Visitors' Association Library, London.

Robson, P. (1982). Health visiting — a brief history. *Radical Health Visitor*; 4.

Rosenthal, H. (1980). *Health and Community Work — Some New Approaches.* Paper commissioned for the King's Fund, London Community Health Resource, London.

Royal College of Nursing, Health Visitors' Advisory Group (1982). *Thinking about Health Visiting.* RCN, London.

Salvage, J. (1985). *The Politics of Nursing.* Heinemann, London.

Smith, C. (1982). *Community Based Health Initiatives: A Handbook for Community Groups.* Bedford Square Press/National Council for Voluntary Organisations, London.

Somerville, G. (1985). *Addressing the Confusions.* King's Fund Centre, London.

Spicer, F. (1980). A support group for health visitors. *Health Visitor*; **53**: 377–9.

Spray, J. (1982). The political naïvity of health visitors. *Radical Health Visitor Group Newsletter*; 6.

Thomas, D. (1983). *The Making of Community Work.* Allen & Unwin, London.

Thomas, P., Sullivan, A. (1983). A mothers' and babies group in a family health clinic. *Health Visitor*; **56**: 299–300.

Thunhurst, C. (1982). *It Makes you Sick: the Politics of the NHS.* Pluto Press, London.

Torkington, P. (1983). *The Racial Politics of Health — a Liverpool Profile*. Department of Sociology, University of Liverpool, Liverpool.

Townsend, P. (1979). *Poverty in the United Kingdom*. Penguin, Middlesex.

Tyler, M., Barnes, S. (1986). A group approach to living with stress. *Health Visitor*; **59**: 14–16.

Vizard, E. (1983). 20 months of Fridays. *Health Visitor*; **56**: 255–6.

Walters, M. (1979). Post-natal support. *Health Visitor*; **52**: 416–7.

Wann, M. (1984). Community health visiting. *London Health News*; May: 12.

Whitehead, M. (1987). *The Health Divide*. Health Education Council, London.

Wilson, T., Jenkins, S. (1985). *The Health of Homeless Families*. Unpublished. St. Mary's Hospital Medical School, London.

World Health Organization (1974). *Community Health Nursing*: Report of a WHO expert committee. WHO, Geneva.

World Health Organization (1978). *Primary Health Care (Declaration of Alma Alta)*. WHO, Geneva.

World Health Organization (1981). *Global Strategy for Health for all by the Year 2000*. WHO, Geneva.

Wynn-Williams, C. (1986). *Personal Communication*. Granton Community Health Project, Edinburgh.

Youd, L., Jayne, L. (1987) *The First Three Years*. Salford Community Health Project, Salford.

Yudkin, J. (1978). Changing patterns of resource allocation in a London teaching district. *British Medical Journal*; 28 October; **2**: 1212–5.

Zola, I. (1975). Medicine as an institution of social control. In: Cox, C., Mead, A. (eds.) *A Sociology of Medical Practice*. Collier Macmillan, London.

Useful Reading

SOCIAL STATISTICS

Central Statistical Office (Annual). *Social Trends*. HMSO, London.
Fothergill, S., Vincent, J. (1985). *The State of the Nation*. Heinemann, London.
Graham, H. (1984). *Women, Health and the Family*. Wheatsheaf Books, Sussex.
National Children's Home (1987). *Children in Danger. An NCH Factfile About Children Today*. National Children's Home, London.
Osman, T. (1985). *The Facts of Everyday Life*. Faber & Faber, London.

HEALTH AND THE HEALTH SERVICES

Black, N., Boswell, D., Gray, A., Murphy, S., Popay, J. (eds.) (1984). *Health and Disease: A Reader*. Open University Press, Milton Keynes.
Butler, J., Vaile, M. (1984). *Health and Health Services: an Introduction to Health Care in Great Britain*. Routledge & Kegan Paul, London.
Doyal, L. (1979). *The Political Economy of Health*. Pluto Press, London.
Mares, P., Henley, A., Baxter, C. (1985). *Health Care in Multiracial Britain*. Health Education Council/National Extension College, London.
Mitchell, J. (1984). *What is to be Done about Illness and Health?* Penguin, Middlesex.
Salvage, J. *The Politics of Nursing*. Heinemann, London.

Townsend, P., Davidson, N. (1982). *Inequalities in Health: The Black Report*. Pelican Books, Middlesex.
Whitehead, M. (1987). *The Health Divide: Inequalities in Health in the 1980s*. Health Education Council, London.

COMMUNITY HEALTH INITIATIVES

CHIRU/LCHR (1987). *A Guide to Community Health Projects*. CHIRU/LCHR, London.
Kenner, C. (1986). *Whose Needs Count?* Bedford Square Press, London.
McNaught, A. (1988). *Health Action and Ethnic Minorities*. Bedford Square Press, London.
Smith, C. (1982). *Community Based Health Initiatives: A Handbook For Community Groups*. National Council for Voluntary Organisations, London.
Somerville, G. (ed.) (1985). *Addressing The Confusions: Community Development in Health*. The King's Fund, London.

GROUP WORK

Brandes, D., Phillips, H. (1978). *Gamesters' Handbook*. Hutchinson, London.
Douglas, T. (1978). *Basic Groupwork*. Tavistock Publications, London.
Falshaw, M. (1985). *Self-Help Learning Groups: A Practical Guide For Organisers*. National Extension College, Cambridge.
Lever, M. et al. (1985). *A Guide to Running Informal Learning Groups*. National Extension College, Cambridge.
Pinder, C. (1985). *Community Start Up: How To Start a Community Group and Keep it Going*. National Extension College, Cambridge.
Richardson, A. (1984). *Working with Self Help Groups: A Guide for Local Professionals*. Bedford Square, Press, London.
Satow, A., Evans, M. (Undated). *Working with Groups*. Health Education Council/Tacade, London.

Useful Videos on Groups

Working with Groups (Undated). Health Education Council/Tacade. (This is a training video to accompany the booklet by Satow and Evans referred to above.)
Time to Act (1984). Health Education Council/Age Concern. (This shows a number of pensioners' health groups.)
Well Woman Series 1–6 (1982). BBC. (Each episode shows a different women's health group.)

IDEAS FOR GROUP WORK IN HEALTH

Age Well Campaign (1986). *Age Well Ideas Pack.* Health Education Council/Age Concern.
Age Well Campaign (1986). *Health and Retirement: Ideas and Resources.* University of London Department of Extramural Studies/Health Education Council.
Black, D., Laughlin, S. (eds.) (1979). *Unemployment and Health Resource Pack.* Greater Glasgow Health Board Health Education Department,Glasgow.
Clarity Collective (British edition by Dixon, H., Mullinar, G.) (1983). *Taught not Caught: Strategies for Sex Education.* Learning Development Aids.
Greater Glasgow Health Board Health Education Department (Undated). *Women's Health Fair, Glasgow.* Glasgow Health Education Department, Glasgow.
Homans, H., Aggleton, P., Warwick, I. (1987). *Learning about AIDS.* Health Education Authority/AVERT.
Kenner, C. (1985). *No Time for Women.* Pandora Press, London.
Lothian Health Board Health Education Department (1987). *Women and Well Being Pack.* Lothian Health Board Health Education Department, Lothian.
Meade, K. (1986). *Challenging the Myths.* Age Well Campaign, Age Concern, Surrey.
National Extension College (1987). *Health Matters — The YTS Health Education Resource Pack.* National Extension College/ Health Education Council.
Pensioners' Link Health Education Project (1987). *Helping Yourself To Health.* Age Well Campaign, Age Concern, Surrey.
Sziron, T., Dyson, S. (British edition by Slavin, S.) (1986). *Greater Expectations: a Source Book for Working with Girls.* Learning Development Aids.

Workers Education Association, North West District Health Education for Women Project (1987). *Women and Health Teaching Pack*. WEA Publications, London.

PRACTICAL RESOURCES

Ewles, L., Simnett, I. (1985). *Promoting Health: A Practical Guide to Health Education*. John Wiley, Chichester.
Health Education Authority (regularly updated). *Source Lists*. HEA.
Mansfield Community Health Project (1986). *A Mobile Crêche*. Mansfield Community Health Project, Community House, 36 Wood St, Mansfield, Notts. NG18 1QA.
Munro, J., Loeb, D. (1986). *Audio-Visuals for Community Groups*. Community Projects Foundation, London.
Paddington and North Kensington Health Promotion Unit (1983). *Health Education Resources on Women's Health*. Paddington and North Kensington Health Promotion Unit (2nd edn. due published 1988).

NEWSLETTERS

National Community Health Resource, 15 Britannia Street, London WC1X 9JP. This newsletter and bulletin includes up-to-date information about community health groups, resources and related issues.
Radical Community Medicine, 55 Fairbridge Road, London N19 3EW. A quarterly journal concerned about promoting public health by changing the practice of community medicine. It has a useful information and network section.
Women's Health and Reproductive Rights Information Centre, 52 Featherstone St, London EC1Y 8RT. This newsletter includes a variety of articles, often on a particular aspect of women's health, and has information about related community groups.

Index

time allocation, 23
training, 23–5
working with others, 59–61
workshops, 99–107
Health Visitors' Association
   (HVA), 8, 16, 18, 109, 111, 112
Homeless, health care for, 5, 79–89
Housing Act (1977), 79

Income levels statistics, 4
Infant welfare clinics, 14
Inner City Partnership, 71
Institute of Marital Studies, 95

King's Fund Centre, 101
Korner recommendations (1983),
   22

Ladies Sanitary Association, 14
London Community Health
   Resource (LCHR), 12

Migration trends, 2

National Health Service (NHS):
   attitudes, 17, 108
   changes in, 5–6
Networking, 114–17
Nurses, as health visitors, 24

Old age health patterns, 5

Parents' Groups, 83–5
Planning group meetings, 127–32
Political involvement, 22, 109
Population change statistics, 2
Practitioners' Skills Exchange, 36
Pre-School Playgroups
   Association, 83

Racism and health effects, 5
Radical Health Visitors' Group
   (RHVG), 8, 16, 108–13
Riverside child health project,
   69–78
Royal College of Nursing (RCN)
   attitudes to group work, 19

Save the Children Fund, 71
Social class factors, 41
Social control role, 20–1
Social pattern changes, 2–3

Tranquilliser support group, 47–52

Under-5's group, 83–5
Unemployment patterns, 3, 5

Work patterns, 3
Workshops, 99–107
   Bangladeshi community project,
      100–2
   East Tower Hamlets, 104–7
World Health Organisation
   (WHO), 8